The Majority Press

LITERARY GARVEYISM: Garvey, Black Arts and the Harlem Renaissance

TONY MARTIN established himself as the leading scholar of the Garvey Movement with his *Race First: The Ideological and Organizational Struggles of Marcus Garvey and the Universal Negro Improvement Association* (1976). He followed this up with *The Pan-African Connection* (1983). He also co-authored *Rare Afro-Americana: A Reconstruction of the Adger Library* (1981).

Martin is professor and chairman of the Black Studies Department at Wellesley College, Massachusetts. He did his M.A. and Ph.D. in history at Michigan State University and the B.Sc. in economics at the University of Hull, England. In 1965 he qualified as a barrister-at-law at Gray's Inn, London. He has taught at the University of Michigan - Flint, the Cipriani Labor College (Trinidad) and St. Mary's College (Trinidad). He has been visiting professor at the University of Minnesota and Brandeis University.

THE NEW MARCUS GARVEY LIBRARY

A Series of Original Works by TONY MARTIN

No. 1.   Literary Garveyism: Garvey, Black Arts and the Harlem Renaissance

No. 2.   The Poetical Works of Marcus Garvey

No. 3.   Marcus Garvey, Hero: A First Biography

No. 4.   Amy Ashwood Garvey: Pan-Africanist, Feminist and Wife No. 1

No. 5.   African Fundamentalism: A Literary Anthology of the Garvey Movement

No. 6.   The Pan-African Connection: From Slavery to Garvey and Beyond

No. 7.   Message to the People: The Course of African Philosophy (By Marcus Garvey. Ed. by Tony Martin)

No. 8.   Race First: The Ideological and Organizational Struggles of Marcus Garvey and the Universal Negro Improvement Association

No. 9.   The Philosophy and Opinions of Marcus Garvey (Ed. by Amy Jacques Garvey. Preface by Tony Martin)

LITERARY GARVEYISM

Garvey, Black Arts and the Harlem Renaissance

TONY MARTIN

The New Marcus Garvey Library, No. 1

THE MAJORITY PRESS
Dover, Massachusetts

Library of Congress Cataloging in Publication Data

Martin, Tony, 1942 -
  Literary Garveyism.

  (The New Marcus Garvey library ; no. 1)
  Bibliography : p.
  Includes index.
  1. American literature--Afro-American authors--
History and criticism. 2. American literature--20th cen-
tury--History and criticism. 3. American literature--New
York (N.Y.)--History and criticism. 4. Garvey, Marcus,
1887-1940. 5. Afro-American arts--New York (N.Y.) 6.
Harlem Renaissance. 7. Afro-Americans--Race identity. 8.
Black nationalism--History. I. Title. II. Series : Martin,
Tony, 1942-   New Marcus Garvey library ;
no. 1.
PS 153.N5M263 1983   810'.9'896073   83-60952
ISBN 0-912469-00-5
ISBN 0-912469-01-3 (pbk.)

First published in 1983, simultaneously in hardbound and
paperback volumes.

 9 8 7 6 5 4

The Majority Press
P. O. Box 538
Dover, Massachusetts 02030
Printed in the United States of America

To Carter G. Woodson, J.A.
Rogers and Hubert H. Harrison

The funeral of John Edward Bruce, August 1924 - Arthur A. Schomburg, second from right; Marcus Garvey, third from right; Mrs. Florence Bruce, fourth from right, front row.

Contents

	Preface	ix
1	Garvey, Black Arts, Harlem Renaissance	1
2	The Garvey Aesthetic	8
3	Garveyism and Literature	25
4	Poetry for the People	43
5	Book Reviews	91
6	Music, Drama, Art and Elocution	106
7	The Defectors -- Eric Walrond and Claude McKay	124
8	Garvey the Poet	139
9	Conclusion	156
	Notes	165
	Bibliography	187
	Index	193

Preface

Garvey studies have expanded marvellously over the last few years. New books, dissertations and articles have revealed the impressive scope of Marcus Garvey's influence in Africa and the Caribbean. Local studies have been published on the Universal Negro Improvement Association's impact on communities from Buffalo to Los Angeles, Trinidad to South Africa. Garveyism's religious aspect has been highlighted. The ideological content of the movement has been clarified. Work has appeared, or is in the offing, on hitherto neglected members of the Garvey machine, such as Henrietta Vinton Davis and Amy Ashwood Garvey, the first wife of a fleeting marriage.

And yet, Garvey scholarship unfolds only to reveal vast new areas for fresh inquiry. For there seem to be few areas in the lives of African peoples that remained untouched by the onrush of Garveyism in the 1920s.

The present volume propels Garvey studies into a new direction - a direction which, it can be confidently predicted, will prove surprising to many. For if the main argument put forward here is right, then a lot of people have in the past been wrong. This study argues no less than that the Garvey Movement has to be elevated to a position of major importance in the literary epoch of what is popularly known as the Harlem Renaissance. This study shows that Garvey's *Negro World* weekly had a purely literary and artistic influence on masses of people, probably exceeding that of the *Crisis*, *Opportunity* and *Messenger* magazines combined.

In the process the Garvey movement articulated a Black aesthetic quite different from that usually associated with the Renaissance - an aesthetic with a strangely contemporary ring, given its affinity with the Black Arts Movement of the 1960s.

Several leading lights of the Renaissance, Zora Neale Hurston and Eric Walrond among them, were graduates of the *Negro World*, though they did not always advertise this fact. Arthur Schomburg and J.A. Rogers were among its frequent contributors. Major and minor political figures, from Grenada to Ghana, waxed poetic in its pages. In its literary contest of 1921 and its regular book review section, it blazed a trail where its more vaunted rivals had to be content to follow. And above all, it provided an artistic outlet for hundreds of New Negroes whose voices might otherwise have been lost to posterity. The *Negro World* represented the artistic voice of a generation in a way that its rivals could not.

This book may have remained the brief preface to a compilation of Garvey's poems that it originally was, had I not been challenged by the incisive criticism of Professors Henry Louis Gates, Jr. and John Blassingame of Yale University. For this I thank them sincerely. Once upon a time, a long time ago, Richard Newman, then of G.K. Hall and Company, accepted this work in principle. This was before the work outgrew the company. I thank him sincerely. This is neither the first nor the last of my works to benefit greatly from the kind cooperation of librarians in many libraries. I thank them all sincerely, and especially the reference librarians at the Clapp Library of Wellesley

College and the Schomburg Center for Research in Black Culture.

I would like to thank the Association for the Study of Afro-American Life and History for permission to reprint a section of my article, "Carter G. Woodson and Marcus Garvey" *(Negro History Bulletin*, Vol. 40, No. 6, November-December 1977); and also the Collection of American Literature, Beinecke Rare Book and Manuscript Library, Yale University for permission to quote from "The Emperor Effaces Himself" by Zora Neale Hurston. I would like to thank, finally, Harper and Row, Publishers, Inc., for permission to quote from " Yet Do I Marvel" from *On These I Stand* by Countee Cullen; copyright 1925 by Harper and Row, Publishers, Inc.; renewed 1953 by Ida M. Cullen.

Wellesley, Massachusetts
February 1983

Garvey, Black Arts, Harlem Renaissance

During the 1960s, the Civil Rights and Black Power movements gave birth to a flowering of literary activity which came to be known as the Black Arts Movement. Poets and playrights especially attracted a mass following for literary activity which astounded most observers. Large audiences, sometimes numbering in the thousands, flocked to street theatres in Harlem, poetry readings on campuses and the performances of community workshops. For a time recorded poetical works competed with soul music on the best selling charts. Black publishing houses, such as Broadside Press in Detroit and Third World Press in Chicago, were enabled to establish a toehold in an industry which, both before and since, has been among the most difficult for Black enterprise to break into.

Almost all commentators, both Black and white, considered this mass interest in Black poetry and literature to be a phenomenon without precedent. Even the Harlem Renaissance of the 1920s seemed less than an adequate precedent. For it was widely believed, and not without justification, that the Harlem Renaissance was more of an elite and less of a grassroots affair. Furthermore, the leading lights of the 1920s had often relied overwhelmingly on white patronage and largely on a white audience. The major figures of the Black Arts Movement, however, were inclined to espouse Black nationalism and tried harder to mobilize the resources of their own community.

It was during the period of the Black Arts Movement that the Black world rediscovered Marcus Garvey in a big

way. He had never really been forgotten, but during the
1960s and '70s he again became an object of mass interest
which threatened to rival in intensity his heyday of the
1920s. Such was inevitable, for in Garvey's Universal
Negro Improvement Association (UNIA), the generation of
the 1960s found a fitting precursor to its own actions.
Garvey, too, had tried to mobilize the Black world's
resources in its own behalf. Garvey, too, had preached
race pride, community control, self-reliance and, in a
word, Black nationalism. And Garvey had done so with
unparallelled success. The Black Arts Movement,
therefore, looked to Garvey for political inspiration. What
it mostly did not know, was that Garvey could also have
provided literary inspiration. For Garvey, too, half a
century earlier, had demonstrated the fact which so
surprised the commentators of the 1960s - the fact that the
Black masses can be moved to an appreciation for
literature and the arts on a scale not often equalled in
other communities.

Garvey built the largest Pan-African mass organization
of all time. His Universal Negro Improvement Association
by the mid-1920s, boasted over eleven hundred branches
in over forty countries in North, South and Central
America, the Caribbean, Africa, Europe and Australia.[1]

Garvey was born in St. Ann's Bay, Jamaica, on August
17, 1887. Despite a lack of sustained formal schooling
beyond his early teens, he nevertheless managed to
develop a lasting taste for things literary. He read widely
in his father's library (a rare privilege for a poor youth
growing up in 19th century rural Jamaica) and spent all of
his teenage years as first a printer's apprentice and later
as a printer. These early experiences ensured him a
constant supply of reading material.

By the time he moved to the capital city, Kingston, at

the age of sixteen, he was ready to expand his literary interests into new directions. He took elocution lessons and entered public speaking contests. In 1910 he placed third in an islandwide oratorical competition. At the end of the first round, which consisted of a poetical reading, Garvey occupied first place. He fared less well on the prose reading which occupied the second round.[2]

It was about this time that Garvey also began his lifelong career as a journalist, first in Jamaica and later in Costa Rica, Panama, England, the United States, Jamaica again and England for a second time.[3] Many of his poems would eventually first appear in his own publications.

Garvey wandered through Central and South America from 1910 to 1912 and through Britain and Europe from 1912 to 1914. In England he worked for the *Africa Times and Orient Review*, edited by the African, Dusé Mohamed Ali, and one of the best literary and political magazines in the Black world of that time.

Four years of world travel convinced Garvey of the need for founding a racial uplift organization. The result was the UNIA, organized a few days after his return to Jamaica in the summer of 1914. Literature and the arts played an important role in the organization from the very start. Throughout 1914 and 1915 regular meetings and concerts featured debates, oratorical contests, poetry readings, dramatic productions and musical performances. The early UNIA was practically an uplift organization and literary and debating club all rolled into one. And even though Garvey had not yet begun his great North American undertaking, his Jamaican organization was already evincing an interest in Afro-American artistic endeavor. At one early UNIA meeting Amy Ashwood (later to become the first Mrs. Garvey) recited from the works of Paul Laurence Dunbar, Afro-America's most

celebrated poet of the period. Garvey had met the
seventeen year old Amy Ashwood, not insignificantly, at
the weekly meeting of a Kingston literary and debating
society.[4]

In his earliest extant pamphlet, *A Talk With Afro-West
Indians*, published in Jamaica in 1915, Garvey again
demonstrated his interest in the writings (especially
historical) of the Black world's leading men of letters,
among them the West Indian born West African
statesman, Edward Wilmot Blyden and Afro-America's
W.E.B. DuBois (later to become a bitter foe of Garvey). By
this time Garvey had also read, and was in correspondence
with, Booker T. Washington.[5]

It was Washington who encouraged Garvey to journey
to the United States. Washington died before the trip
could take place, but Garvey nevertheless arrived in New
York on March 23, 1916. He hoped to go on a fundraising
tour and return to Jamaica. But such was not to be. One
thing led to another and he was destined, within a mere
three short years, to become one of the best known
Africans in the world.

In the meantime he toured the United States lecturing
and establishing contacts. Some of these contacts were
literary. For his earliest known Afro-American journal
article, "The West Indies in the Mirror of Truth," was
published in January 1917 in the Chicago based *Champion*
magazine, edited by Fenton Johnson. Johnson was one of
Afro-America's better known literary figures. Alain Locke
called him a "pioneer and pathbreaker" of the Harlem
Renaissance.[6]

Two and a half years after arriving in New York, in the
fall of 1918, Garvey established what was soon to become
the crowning achievement of his journalistic career. This
was the weekly *Negro World* newspaper, published in

Harlem. The paper's circulation grew in time to about 200,000 and it enjoyed a worldwide distribution unequalled by any other contemporary Afro-American publication. Garvey himself was the paper's first editor, but his political activity kept him much too busy to serve as full time editor for long. To help him in this task he attracted a succession of Afro-America's leading journalistic and literary figures. Between 1920 and 1927 (the year of Garvey's deportation to Jamaica after conviction on a trumped up charge of mail fraud) the editors, associate editors and literary editors of the *Negro World* included the following luminaries - William H. Ferris, historian, literary critic and graduate of Harvard and Yale; Hubert H. Harrison, perhaps Harlem's best known and most respected intellectual; Eric D. Walrond, a major short story writer of the Harlem Renaissance; T. Thomas Fortune, the "dean of Afro-American journalists," veteran Republican Party activist and former aide to Booker T. Washington; and John Edward Bruce, founder in 1911 of the Negro Society for Historical Research, and a man whose journalistic and political credentials rivalled those of Fortune.

By 1920, two years after its inception, the *Negro World* was already well on its way to becoming the focal point of a mass preoccupation with the arts, especially poetry, unequalled by any of the better-known publications of the Harlem Renaissance. The *Negro World's* role in this was so great that one does not easily understand the near total silence on this subject in practically all of the works on the Harlem Renaissance. Garvey occasionally receives credit in these works for planting the political seeds of race consciousness and Pan-Africanism, both of which saw ample literary expression in the Renaissance. Almost never is it realized that he also had an important direct

impact on the purely literary aspects of the Renaissance as
well.

Yet, some of the leading figures of the period
acknowledged Garvey's literary contribution, however
grudgingly. Among these were the editors of the
Messenger magazine, A. Philip Randolph and Chandler
Owen. This socialist-oriented Black publication is often
considered to have been one of the more important
journalistic contributors to the Harlem Renaissance. Its
editors, like much of Afro-America's integrationist
establishment, led a virulent "Marcus Garvey Must Go"
campaign in the early 1920s.[7] Yet, in the midst of this
campaign in 1922, the *Messenger* could state that

> In spite of all this, Garvey has done much good work in
> putting into many Negroes a backbone where for years
> they have had only a wishbone. He has stimulated race
> pride. He has instilled a feeling into Negroes that they are
> as good as anybody else. He has criticized the hat-in-hand
> Negro leadership. He has inspired an interest in Negro
> traditions, Negro history, Negro literature, Negro art and
> culture. He has stressed the international aspect of the
> Negro problem.[8]

Charles S. Johnson, one of the most celebrated mentors of
the Black authors and artists of the period and editor of
Opportunity magazine, paid a similar, perhaps more
hesitant, tribute to Garvey in Alain Locke's 1925 anthology, *The New Negro*. He saw Garvey as one who
"merely had the clairvoyance to place himself at the head
of" an "awakening black peasantry" and other segments
of an Afro-American population who were tired of "a
culture which has but partially (and again unevenly)
digested the Negro masses - the black peasants least of
all."[9]

But it was Claude McKay who came closest of the

outstanding Renaissance figures to doing justice to Garvey's artistic contributions to the period. McKay carried on a love-hate relationship with the Garvey Movement for years. He wrote in 1940, the year of Garvey's death, that

> Garvey assembled an exhibition of Negro accomplishment in all the skilled crafts, and art work produced by exhibitors from all the Americas and Africa, which were revelations to Harlem of what the Negro people were capable of achieving.
>
> The vivid, albeit crude, paintings of the Black Christ and the Black Virgin of the African Orthodox Church[10] were startling omens of the Negro Renaissance movement of the nineteen twenties, which whipped up the appetite of literary and artistic America for a season. The flowering of Harlem's creative life came in the Garvey era. The anthology, THE NEW NEGRO, which oriented the debut of the Renaissance writers, was printed in 1925. If Marcus Garvey did not originate the phrase, New Negro, he at least made it popular.[11]

Even this assessment fell far short of adequately describing Garvey's contribution to the literary efflorescence of the 1920s. But it was as close as anybody came.

The artistic contribution of Garvey and the *Negro World* may have been even greater, had not the work of the UNIA been hindered from 1923 to 1927 by Garvey's trial, imprisonment and deportation. Yet some good was salvaged from these vicissitudes, for it was in prison that Garvey wrote much of his own poetry.

2

The Garvey Aesthetic

However great his interest in art, Garvey was still a political figure. And art, for him, had to serve the cause of freedom, justice and equality. His view of the place of art in his people's struggle was a succinct statement of what, in the 1960s, came to be known as the "Black aesthetic." "We must encourage our own black authors who have character," Garvey postulated, "who are loyal to their race, who feel proud to be black, and in every way let them feel that we appreciate their efforts to advance our race through healthy and decent literature." [1]

This did not mean that the Black author must necessarily confine himself solely to racial themes. Garvey himself did not do so. His own poetry included items on racially neutral topics. Yet, the briefest of glances through any collection of Garvey's poetry would clearly indicate what his primary concern was.

There was considerable debate within the columns of the *Negro World* over this question of the Black aesthetic. Most contributors tended to follow Garvey's view of art as a weapon in the struggle for African advancement. But the occasional dissenting voice was not unheard of. In this regard the *Negro World* simply mirrored the vexing controversy that raged throughout the 1920s and beyond, among Black artists in general.

Marion S. Lakey, one of the better *Negro World* poets, reflected Garvey's view in a 1922 poem entitled "Mission"-

> I'm struggling far afield today,
>   Son of a lowly race ;

Fortune her gifts must yield to me
　In spite of my black face.
I'm fighting my people's cause today
　To down an ancient wrong,
And to lift this yearning race of mine
　In lofty tale and song.[2]

Garvey's concern with encouraging "our own black authors who have character" implied, of course, that the race should itself decide who its worthy artists were. "We must inspire a literature and promulgate a doctrine of our own," he wrote, "without any apologies to the powers that be. The right is ours and God's. Let contrary sentiment and cross opinions go to the winds." This was in his powerfully eloquent essay on "African Fundamentalism."[3]

John Edward Bruce echoed Garvey's concern. He argued that Afro-America too often refused to accept its literary figures until they had received a stamp of approval from the dominant race. Writing on "The Negro in Poetry" in the *Negro World* in 1923, he stated that those Black poets who "have achieved any distinction, owe it to the fact that some white author, more liberal than is usual, has put the seal of his approval upon their work and thus given them prestige and standing, which they could not otherwise have got. Thus [Paul Laurence] Dunbar jumped into fame at almost a single bound. He came to his own, but his own received him not. William Dean Howells recognized his ability and with a stroke of his pen gave him international fame." Bruce lamented this abdication of responsibility on the part of the Black public. The white man, he said, "designates our poets, political leaders and moral advisers. We accept the designees...."[4]

The problem that Bruce described was well illustrated in the case of Claude McKay, arguably the best poet of the Harlem Renaissance. McKay's first breakthroughs into print in North America came via the white publications, *Seven Arts* (1917) and *Pearson's Magazine* (1918). The poem, "The White Fiends," which Pearson's printed had earlier been rejected by W.E.B. DuBois' *Crisis*, organ of the National Association for the Advancement of Colored People. A selection of his poems had also previously been rejected by William Stanley Braithwaite, Black literary critic for the white Boston *Evening Transcript*.[5] McKay's career, from his early days in Jamaica, was characterized by a succession of white mentors, godfathers and bankrollers. Perhaps DuBois and Braithwaite, in rejecting his work, lost an opportunity for Afro-America to corral one who should have been its own. For McKay, as will be seen, never could fully reconcile himself to the role of race man, his excellent racial poetry notwithstanding. His novel, *Home to Harlem*, caused Garvey in 1928 to place him among those guilty of "prostituting their intelligence, under the direction of the white man, to bring out and show up the worst traits of our people...." The book was, in Garvey's view, "a damnable libel against the Negro."[6]

During the late 1930s, Garvey, now living in England, kept up a similar barrage of criticism against Paul Robeson, by then one of the world's best known actors on stage and screen. He considered Robeson a good actor but a poor representative of his race. Robeson, like McKay, he accused of being manipulated by whites, this time in the playing of racially demeaning roles.[7]

One of Robeson's films, *Emperor Jones*, had been the subject of *Negro World* upset since its first appearance on Broadway in 1920. Written by white playright, Eugene O'Neill, it originally starred Charles Gilpin in the title role of an ex-convict turned buffoonish emperor of a Caribbean island. William Bridges, editor of the *Challenge* and a regular contributor to the *Negro World*, called the *Emperor Jones* a travesty of the African race.[8] Hubert H.

Harrison surprisingly wrote a very favorable review of the
play. He was taken to task by a *Negro World* reader, Mrs.
William A. Corbi of Cambridge, Massachusetts.

Mrs. Corbi's letter illustrates the willingness of the
Negro World to engage in real debate, even when the
paper's own editors came out on the losing end. On this
occasion it was Mrs. Corbi, the reader, who found herself
articulating the correct Garveyite aesthetic as against one
of the *Negro World's* own editors. She wrote,

> Mr. Eugene O'Neill's so-called wonderful play,
> described as a study of the psychology of fear and of race
> superstition, which Mr. Harrison so readily commends to
> Negroes as a work of genius, cannot and will not be ac-
> cepted by race-loving Negroes as a work of genius. Surely
> "Something is rotten in Denmark" when Hubert Harrison
> lauds "Emperor Jones." That is the trouble with our
> educated and intelligent men. They are using their brains
> to keep down their own race.

Harrison had expressed surprise that such a serious play
could succeed so well on Broadway. To Mrs. Corbi, this
fact was not surprising at all. The reason was the same as
that which had made the film *Birth of a Nation* a success.
For, she informed Harrison,

> Anything that causes the white man to believe that the
> Negroes are superstitious, immoral and illiterate...can
> make a hit on Broadway....
> One does not need "an understanding of drama and its
> laws," to quote Mr. Harrison, to realize that "Emperor
> Jones" is of no racial value to the Negroes of the World.
> The play does not elevate the Negro, and such plays never
> will.

Mrs. Corbi ended with parting shots against Harrison,
Gilpin and white writers -

> Such men as Mr. Harrison who encourage white
> playrights by lauding them to the skies, are of no racial
> value to the Negroes. Remember always the man who
> allows a man to make a fool of him will always be a fool.
> Charles Gilpin has won fame in "Emperor Jones." Now
> let them bring him back in one of the higher plays, and see
> how long he will remain on the great white way.
>
> The time has come when Negroes will not accept such
> plays as great. Let the white man write them of himself
> and the Negroes will say "Atta Boy."[9]

Ten years after the Harrison-Corbi exchange another
Negro World editor became involved in a similar difference of opinion. This time editor H.G. Mudgal praised
the *Pittsburgh Courier* for its campaign against the
"insulting" radio comedy show, "Amos 'n' Andy," where
white actors portrayed two dimwitted Black characters.
Arthur S. Gray, a regular *Negro World* contributor,
disagreed with Mudgal. He thought that the show was to
be laughed off, rather than to be upset over.[10]

For most commentators within and without the *Negro
World*, the question of a Black aesthetic was usually raised
in the form of debate on the place of "propaganda" in art.
Art consciously enlisted in the cause of struggle was
considered by some to be mere propaganda and not
worthy of true art. Those of Garvey's persuasion saw
"propaganda" as a desirable element in art, if art was to
have any purpose.

The *Negro World* in 1920 praised the advent of the
Promoter magazine, edited by a regular contributor,
Hodge Kirnon. The magazine was "radical and racial at
the same time," and therefore good.[11] At times the Black
artist might suffer in terms of recognition and wider short
term critical acclaim because of a propagandist stance.
But this was not an unreasonable price to ask of the
racially committed. Marion S. Lakey made this point in a

1923 critique of the work of fellow *Negro World* poet, Ethel Trew Dunlap. He wrote, "One comes to realize more and more as one reads Miss Dunlap's poems that it will be the women of the race who will lead the race to a higher and more genuinely cultured spiritual plane....Miss Dunlap is - yes - a poetess laureate and a heroine to her race, in that she has dared to write for a cause that means everything to the future well-being of her race at a time when that cause is the object of the supercilious ridicule and contempt of many of her own people, thus, to a certain extent, sacrificing for the time her chance to win a larger but what could not be other than a less altruistic fame."[12]

Even among those who favored propaganda, however, there were different shades of emphasis. *Negro World* literary editor, William H. Ferris, consistently advocated a subtle and understated propaganda. Propaganda that was too strident and preachy might, in his view, detract from the niceties of plot, characterization and style that went to make, say, a good novel. By some strange dialectical process, the masterfully written, subtly propagandistic novel would be a much more powerful weapon than a strident, poorly constructed work. "The Novel," he argued, "has been a potent method of arousing the public conscience. Harriet Beecher Stowe's 'Uncle Tom's Cabin' won more converts to the slave's cause than did the brilliant addresses of Sumner, Phillips and Douglass and the forceful editorials of Garrison." It followed from this argument that the task facing the Black novelist of the 1920s was to create great fiction - "Novels which can powerfully picture the civilization of Africa during the Middle Ages, novels which can powerfully envisage the struggles of an aspiring Negro in a hostile Anglo-Saxon civilization, will undoubtedly add to the prestige and standing of the Negro Race."[13]

If the fiction of the second Mrs. Garvey (Amy Jacques Garvey), is any indication, then Marcus Garvey was less troubled by overt propaganda than was Ferris. Mrs. Garvey was as perfect a companion for her husband as any political leader could hope for - powerful orator, efficient private secretary, excellent editor (she edited his two books of poems and his seminal two volume *Philosophy and Opinions*), sometime associate editor of the *Negro World*, later her husband's biographer and a devoted wife and mother. Garvey certainly could not have asked for more.

In 1923 Amy Jacques Garvey published a short story in the *Negro World* entitled "Whither Goest Thou?" The main character was a Black Mississippian. The man's friend had been lynched and he himself beaten up and thrown unconscious into a train's jim crow coach. A note pinned to his coat advised him to get out of town. He did. He went to Arkansas. But before he could settle down there his host Black community was given twenty-four hours to remove itself. Our protagonist thus found himself involuntarily on the road again, this time to New York. But New York was no place to be cold, penniless, unemployed and destitute. Driven by unfathomable desperation, he decided to commit larceny and turn himself in. In jail at least there would be a warm place to sleep and food to eat. But the judge refused to jail him under these circumstances. He had no choice but to face a hostile world once more, vowing this time to make it to jail by committing "one of the most fiendish robberies" imaginable. Mrs. Garvey ended her story like this -

"The door closed behind him and the blizzard raged before him.

"Negro; whither goest thou?"[14]

This was powerful stuff, though Ferris may have

considered it unsubtle. One aspect of the story of which he would definitely have approved, however, was Mrs. Garvey's starkly realistic treatment of an inelegant theme. For herein lay an element which frequently entered into the debate over propaganda and art. Should the Black writer reveal the joys and sorrows, even the misery and degradation that were to be found among the mass of people, or should he or she emphasize only the genteel and refined?

Ferris opted for the former. His criticism of Black artists here is reminiscent of E. Franklin Frazier's later classic, *Black Bourgeoisie*, which so cruelly exposed the world of make-believe wherein much of the Black middle class has traditionally sought respite from its frustrations. "One of the stumbling blocks in the pathway to Negro progress," Ferris wrote, "is the Negro's false conception of art. Art to him, be it music, poetry, drama, sculpture, painting [or] literature...is a thing that appeals exclusively to the cultural-minded, to the bourgeoisie, to the lords and ladies who try, and fail miserably, to develop a genuine Bohemianism...." Black artists had before them the examples of Shakespeare, Robert Burns, and Paul Laurence Dunbar, all of whom had shown that great art does not have to lose touch with the masses. But they had largely rejected these models. "Instead, by virtue of social pressure, Negro artists are forced to produce works that bring out 'the higher aspirations of the Negro,' works that with a brutally sterile puritanism steer clear of the beauty and simplicity of true art."[15]

Here, however, as with other aspects of the propaganda question, the nuances were finely drawn. For it was one thing to write about ordinary folk, but quite another to hold their foibles up to ridicule in the name of realism. This would explain Garvey's language, previously noted, in reference to Claude McKay's *Home to Harlem*, to the effect that some writers were "prostituting their intelligence, under the direction of the white man, to bring out and show up the worst traits of our people...."[16] The same debate reappeared in the 1970s, over the depiction (some would say glorification) of prostitution, drugs and violence in "Black exploitation" films.

The generality of *Negro World* writers were much more pro- propaganda than most of the better known figures of the Harlem Renaissance. Novelist and poet Jessie Fauset spoke for many of the latter when she urged the Black actor to become "an artist first and only secondarily...a Negro."[17] Inherent in her argument was the supposition that one had to purge oneself of one's identity in order to achieve artistic perfection, a sacrifice which Fauset and her ilk seemed not to require of white artists.

The anti-propaganda school found its only consistent *Negro World* voice in Eric Walrond, an associate editor from 1921 to 1923. For Walrond, propaganda tended to detract from good art. And according to his way of thinking, the propaganda trap was one that the Black writer in the United States was more or less forced into by the prevailing climate of racism. "One reason why the Negro has not made any sort of headway in fiction," he wrote in the *Dearborn Independent*, "is due to the effects of color prejudice. It is difficult for a Negro to write stories without bringing in the race question. As soon as a writer demonstrates skill along imaginative lines he is bound to succumb to the temptation of reform and propaganda."[18] Walrond did not adequately explain why the Black writer should not deal with racism, given, as he himself admitted, that the experience of racism represented the Black writer's most pervasive reality. His position was anomalous within the context of the *Negro World*, and will be discussed later. He came close to the classically a-social stance of art for its own sake. This position received an extreme endorsement from the painter Salvador Dali in 1980 when he said that "nobody knows whether the Venus de Milo was a fascist or a Communist."[19]

The debate over propaganda was a debate over the use of art for positive social ends. Where art was harnessed to the cause of oppression there was little if any disagreement. Even those unwilling to countenance pro-Black propaganda unwittingly acknowledged the power, even of unsubtle propaganda, in their frenzied reactions to the racist novels of, say, a Thomas Dixon. *Negro World* columnist (later editor) H. G. Mudgal in 1922 provided some expressive commentary on the arch propagandist, Rudyard Kipling, the "poet laureate of British imperialism." For him, Kipling was "the only great artist in the history of humanity who has proved capable of misusing his art for dark purposes and destructive ends …." On reflection he even contested Kipling's designation as a "great artist." For Kipling seemed "a stinking carcass with gaudy clothing and fragrant flowers on."[20] It was doubtless with the Rudyard Kiplings of this world in mind that UNIA conventions in New York in 1924 and Jamaica in 1934 suggested a literary censor to safeguard the race from unfavorable literature.[21]

While the pro and anti-propaganda lines may have seemed clear to some in theory, they were often muddled in practice. The fine distinctions drawn in the arguments of the main protagonists made this inevitable. The non - UNIA artists especially, usually exhibited considerable lack of clarity on this question. Sometimes they vacillated between one position and the other. Often they tried to eat their cake and have it too, arguing in theory against propaganda while being unable in practice to escape the all encompassing reality of North American racial prejudice.

For the leading figures of the Harlem Renaissance this confusion was fed in large part by a political fact. Most of them depended on white mentors and/or worked for predominantly white or at least white financed organizations. Thus Claude McKay drifted from one white patron to the next, whether in Jamaica or the United States or Europe. Jessie Fauset worked for W.E.B. DuBois' *Crisis* magazine, the organ of the then white dominated NAACP. William Stanley Braithwaite worked for the white Boston *Evening Transcript*. In the case of Jean Toomer, he could pass for white anytime he felt like and he eventually ended his days as a white Quaker in Pennsylvania. Zora Neale Hurston was significantly helped along by white patrons.

Langston Hughes had his fair share of white mentors, too, but he somehow managed to maintain a more widespread credibility within his community than most of the others. In fact, Amy Jacques Garvey was quite excited by his famous essay on "The Negro Artist and the Racial Mountain." She probably would not have agreed with every single word in it, but there was enough in it to transport her into rapturous joy. Hughes had begun his essay by telling a little story that could easily have been written by a Harrison or a Garvey -

> One of the most promising of the young Negro poets said to me once, "I want to be a poet - not a Negro poet," meaning, I believe, "I want to write like a white poet;" meaning subconsciously "I would like to be a white poet;" meaning behind that, "I would like to be white." And I was sorry the young man said that, for no great poet has ever been afraid of being himself. And I doubted then that, with his desire to run away spiritually from his race, this

boy would ever be a great poet. But this is the mountain standing in the way of any true Negro art in America - this urge within the race toward whiteness, the desire to pour racial individuality into the mold of American standardization, and to be as little Negro and as much American as possible.[22]

Mrs. Garvey was "delighted with the frank statement of Mr. Hughes in a white magazine." She did not know whether he was "a registered member of the Universal Negro Improvement Association," but "in any event his closing paragraph" showed him to be "a keen student of Garveyism, and with stamina enough to express its ideals...." For Hughes had declared therein, "Why should I want to be white? I am a Negro - and beautiful." "Bravo, Mr. Hughes!" Mrs. Garvey rejoiced,"...let the canvas come to life with dark faces; let poetry charm the muses with the hopes and aspirations of our race; let the musicians drown our sorrows with the merry jazz; while a race is in the making, and steadily moving on to nationhood and to power."[23]

Hughes was somewhat of an exception. His fellow luminaries of the Renaissance mainstream more typically tended to follow the dictates, expressed or implied, of their white patrons. Nor were these patrons always reluctant to foist their anti-propaganda ideas onto their Black protégés. Carl Van Vechten, White Patron No. 1, addressed this controversy in his novel, *Nigger Heaven*. In his cold, sometimes incisive, arrogant and presumptuous way, he said of his character Byron, an aspiring young Black writer - "Try as he might, he could not get away from propaganda. The Negro problem seemed to hover over him and occasionally like the great, black bird it was, claw at his heart. In his stories this influence invariably made itself felt, and it was, he was sometimes convinced, the very thing that kept him from doing better work." [24]

White support for major Renaissance figures inevitably brought with it some commitment to an integrationist political perspective. And the anti-propaganda position was, more often than not, an integrationist position. For why use one's artistic gifts on behalf of racial struggle when one's larger purpose was to escape race altogether into a colorless world? Unlike the Garveyite intellectual, Ferris, who argued that great art, à la Shakespeare, Burns and Dunbar, could have universal appeal despite a parochial base, the anti-propagandists of the 1920s were more apt to believe that great art must be "universal" to begin with, in the sense of shedding itelf of its primary sectional appeal.

William Stanley Braithwaite expressed this position very well in comments on Jessie Fauset's novel, *There Is Confusion*, which was set among the Black middle class. The strength of the work lay for him in the fact that it avoided " the limitations of propaganda on the one hand and genre fiction on the other [and therefore] emerges from the color line and is incorporated into the body of general and universal art." Braithwaite liked Jean Toomer's *Cane* even more, since "So objective is it, that we feel that it is a mere accident that birth or association has thrown him into contact with the life he has written about." Toomer, he thought, would write equally well about Irish or Russian peasants if a chance opportunity should bring him into contact with them.[25]

Braithwaite tied his anti-propaganda position very explicitly to his political integrationism, in what sounded like an upside down propagandist position of his own. The task of the Black artist, he said, was to "lift the Negro into the only full and complete nationalism he knows - that of the American democracy."[26]

Yet even so committed an anti-propagandist and integrationist as Braithwaite could exhibit some confusion on this question. Despite his love for the de-racialized Jean Toomer, who could write equally well of Black, Irish or Russian peasants, he could contradictorily assert in the same article that only a Black person could write a really accurate Black novel.[27]

W.E.B. DuBois, always confused and vacillating on things ideological, exhibited this confusion in an acute way. In 1921 he inveighed against the growing tendency among Black artists to "insist that our Art and Propaganda be one." By 1926 he was equally vehement that "All Art is propaganda.... I do not care a damn, for any art that is not used for propaganda."[28] This about face represented the first stirrings of what was eventually to blossom forth into a short lived flirtation with Garvey style separatism.[29]

The contradiction besetting Braithwaite and so many others was that they were drawn into an integrationist position at a time when the Black masses (and some sections of the middle class, too) were giving organizational expression to Black nationalism on an unprecedented scale. For the Garvey Movement, with its 35,000 members in the New York local alone, represented a force from which none could escape. Some fallout from Garvey's insistent message of race pride, self-reliance and African redemption could not help but settle, even on conservative elements within the mainstream of the Harlem Renaissance. This, and the all-embracing nature of North American racism, which refused to release from its grasp even those who would ignore it.

The Garveyite propagandists of course rejected the integrationism espoused by many of the Renaissance leading lights. An unsigned *Negro World* editorial of 1922 (probably written by Ferris), looked forward "to a period when DuBois, James Weldon Johnson and the other high-brow black Americans who think white, will have abandoned the shadow of a spurious American citizenship for the more solid advantages of African co-operation and repatriation."[30]

These conflicting attitudes to propaganda can be observed in the works of other contemporary figures. Claude McKay, for example, could at times be the most powerful of propagandists. Recalling Braithwaite's rejection of his early offerings because they betrayed his race too much, he commented - "Need I say that I did not entertain, not in the least, Mr. Braithwaite's most excellent advice?.... My poetic expression was too subjective, personal and tell-tale.... a discerning person would become immediately aware that I came from a tropical country and that I was not, either by the grace of God or the desire of man, born white." Like Ferris, McKay was aware that many of the world's white literary figures - "Byron, Shelley, Keats, Blake, Burns, Whitman, Heine, Baudelaire, Verlaine and Rimbaud and the rest" - had made no effort to submerge their identities. "In their poetry," he wrote, "I could feel their class, their roots in the soil...."[31]

McKay's propagandism was fuelled not only by considerations of race, but by his few years of flirtation with left wing radicalism. While in the Soviet Union in 1922-23 he was commissioned to write a book on *The Negroes in America*. Here, in an effort to please his communist hosts, appeared perhaps his strongest endorsement of propaganda. "The only [Black] literature which merits any attention," he argued, "is that which has the character of national propaganda. Almost any Negro writer, however much he might appear to be minding his own business, is really drawn into active work in the area of propaganda.

Such a great, urgent need can be felt here that not a single thinking person can stand aloof."[32]

Yet McKay was not entirely without confusion on this question. Recalling later his break with his white colleagues on the radical New York based *Liberator* magazine, he commented, "I cannot be convinced of a proletarian, or a bourgeois, or any special literature or art."[33]

McKay of course wrote excellent propaganda as well as non-propaganda verse. His contemporaries were divided, for the most part along predictable lines, over which they liked better. Robert Lincoln Poston, *Negro World* editorial writer and secretary general of the UNIA, thought that McKay's propaganda poems "for the present....serve a splendid purpose." He harbored the fear, though, that some of McKay's verse might suffer the fate of John Greenleaf Whittier's anti-slavery poetry - future generations with new preoccupations might pass them by.[34] Poet Countee Cullen thought that "Claude McKay is most exercised, rebellious, and vituperative to a degree that clouds his lyricism in many instances, but silhouettes most forcibly his high dudgeon...."[35] Braithwaite seemed to see McKay's propaganda poetry as definitely second best to his "poetry of expression," a temporary, perhaps pardonable aberration into which younger Black poets were invariably drawn. He also saw the fact that McKay wrote both propaganda and neutral poetry to be reflective of a wavering "between the racial and the universal notes."[36] This was not necessarily the case, for an espousal of propaganda did not necessarily carry with it any obligation to refrain from writing about springtime in New Hampshire or Harlem dancers.

Though the anti-propaganda position was mostly confined to integrationists, the converse was obviously not true. Black nationalists, though normally pro-propaganda, obviously did not have any monopoly on this tendency. W.E.B. DuBois, coming out (in the 1920s) of the radical integrationist protest school, arrived in due and roundabout course at a propagandist position, as already seen. His colleague at the NAACP, James Weldon Johnson, though more ambiguous, at least summed up the complexities of the propaganda debate very well. He noted that the Renaissance poets had largely failed to live up to the anti-propaganda rhetoric which many of them preached. Countee Cullen, for instance, might "with justification chafe under any limitation of art to race, for he is a true lyric poet," but yet "the best of his poetry rises out of the idea of race and is permeated with it." He felt the same way about the race poetry of Langston Hughes.[37]

He felt the same way, indeed, about the whole Renaissance generation, whose race poetry seemed to him to be its best. Addressing himself to the whole corpus of Afro-American poetry he observed that "not in all of it do I find a single poem possessing the power and artistic finality found in the best of the poems rising out of racial conflict and contact."[38] History has not diminished the correctness of Johnson's view. Certainly the most famous, most loved and most often quoted poem of the Harlem Renaissance has to be McKay's fighting sonnet, "If We Must Die" - "...If we must die, Oh let us nobly die...."[39]

3

Garveyism and Literature

> ...the UNIA is making a tremendous contribution to the education of the race. In every issue of the Negro World space is given to the aspirants of the race in the realm of literature and poetry. Of course, much of the prose they contribute is amateurish and lacking in etymology and syntax, crude in diction and utterly tawdry; and many of their sample verses are merely doggerels. But... if out of the hundreds that get a literary hearing in the columns of the Negro World just a dozen should make a lasting mark the effort would not have been in vain....

> In the life of Marcus Garvey men have noted the fire of the prophet, the astuteness of the statesman, the conviction of the propagandist, the magnetism of the general, but few men have noted the erudition of the educator.[1]

The author of the above *Negro World* quotation was Arnold Hamilton Maloney, M.A., S.T.D., one time assistant chaplain general of the UNIA, a regular contributor to the paper's columns and a professor of psychology at Wilberforce University in Ohio. He accurately depicted the mass nature of the UNIA literary effort. No other publication of the time, neither *Opportunity*, nor the *Crisis*, nor anything else, came close to the *Negro World* for the sheer magnitude of its literary output. This was compounded by the fact that unlike the more vaunted literary journals of the period, the *Negro World* was a weekly, rather than a monthly publication.

Negro World literary activity peaked during the period 1920-1923, but remained a part of the paper until its demise in 1933. During the early 1920s, as many as dozens

25

of poems, short stories, book reviews, articles of literary
criticism and the like might be found in a single issue of
the paper. The authors might range from major literary
and intellectual figures, like William H. Ferris, Eric
Walrond, Zora Neale Hurston, Arthur A. Schomburg, J.A.
Rogers, Alain Locke, Hubert H. Harrison and John
Edward Bruce, to unknown aspiring writers from Africa,
Afro-America, Canada, Central America, the Caribbean
and any of the myriad places where the UNIA was
established and the paper was read. Though all submissions were not automatically accepted (their great
volume made this impossible, anyway) the emphasis was
clearly on fostering a mass interest in literature and the
arts. And, as Maloney pointed out, one sure way of doing
this was by providing a sympathetic forum for large
numbers of would-be writers.

Maloney contrasted the policy of Marcus Garvey and
the *Negro World* with that of W.E.B. DuBois and the
Crisis magazine. He knew a young and aspiring short
story writer, he said, whose literary efforts were much
applauded in his home town. This young man desired
wider recognition, and so he sent a sample of his work to
"one of the great leaders of the race" (DuBois), in the
hope that the leader would publish it in his magazine if it
proved acceptable.

The leader's response was not only discouraging, but
tactlessly and insensitively so. "This letter was like a wet
blanket used to smother a fire," wrote Maloney, "it was
like a frigid wave of wind congealing the blood. I read the
letter and I sighed, and when I had become sufficiently
composed to speak, I gave expression to this thought -
"God, spare us from this type of leadership, if Thou really
desirest that we shall go forward...." What the race
needed was the kind of leadership that Garvey provided,

"leadership that has a keen and abiding interest in posterity and therefore, endeavors to bring to the fore the latent possiblities of the group."[2]

While many of the *Negro World* writers never achieved recognition outside of the UNIA, this was no necessary reflection on the standard of their writing, which was usually high. Many of the most regular contributors came to the paper with established reputations. Some (for example Eric D. Walrond and Zora Neale Hurston) found in the *Negro World* an important outlet for their apprentice writing and moved on from there to the bright lights of the Harlem Renaissance.

The UNIA and *Negro World* exhibited their literary interests in many other ways besides encouraging aspiring writers. A particularly striking manifestation of this interest lay in the large number of *Negro World* editorials devoted to literary subjects. The *Negro World* was the most highly political of newspapers. Yet it was simultaneously the most literary of newspapers. One is hard put to find another primarily politically oriented newspaper which devoted so much space, even on its editorial pages, to literary concerns. Perhaps it might be an appreciation of René Maran's prize winning novel, *Batouala*; or it might be an attack on the writings of T.S. Stribling, white author of the 1921 novel, *Birthright*, or a discussion of art and propaganda - such was the stuff that many a *Negro World* editorial was made of.

One 1923 editorial, "Adina Revolts," actually took the form of a short story. The heroine, Adina, is a mulatto servant working for a white woman. Adina's sister is pregnant and asks permission for Adina to take nine days off from work immediately following the baby's birth. The mistress refuses, whereupon Adina overcomes her servile position and quits the job. Dignity prevails over economic necessity.[3]

Because the editors tended to be literary men, even their non-literary editorials and other articles were full of literary allusions and poetic quotations. Stylistically, their writing was of a consistently elegant quality. Even such a potentially routine topic as "A Look in Liberty Hall[4] Sunday Night," could not deter editor T. Thomas Fortune from a moving and eloquent composition. He noted on this occasion that the crowd was restless and kept peering towards the main entrance, even though the night's activities were in progress. He soon realized why. Garvey was not there -

> Then I understood. We were having Hamlet with Hamlet left out, and the big audience was not satisfied.
>
> The program dragged along in a humdrum way, with no enthusiasm, but with a wistful looking to the far entrance for the coming of the chief. What a tremendous thing it is to be able to inspire the love and admiration of millions of people, who are not satisfied when you are gone and overwhelm you with affection and attention when you are with them. Only a few men in history have been so blessed, marked men, who have changed the map of the world....
>
> And then, as if he had come right up out of the bottom of nowhere, Marcus Garvey appeared on the platform and faced the assembled host, clothed in the robes of his office, and the vast gathering broke into applause, which sounded like the rush of many waters.[5]

A witty and unusual 1924 editorial by associate editor Norton G. Thomas consisted of a delightful parody of a well-known passage from Shakespeare's *Julius Caesar*. Entitled "With Apologies to Shakespeare," it was in fact a reply to W.E.B. DuBois' notorious *Crisis* polemic characterizing Garvey as a "Lunatic or a Traitor." The editorial opened at "Act XCIX. Scene IX. Harlem Seventh

Avenue" -

> Enter William Pickens, William DuBois and Weldon Johnson.[6]

DuBois (Nervously)

> Another general shout!
> I do believe, that these applauses are
> For some new Honors that are heaped on Garvey.

Johnson

> Why, man, he doth bestride the world of Negroes
> Like a Colossus; and we petty men
> Walk under his huge legs, and peep about
> To find ourselves dishonorable graves,
> Men at some time are masters of their fates;
> The fault, dear DuBois, is not in our stars,
> But in ourselves, that we are underlings.
> DuBois and Garvey: What should be in that Garvey?
> Why should that name be sounded more than yours?
> Write them together, yours is as fair a name;
> Sound them, it doth become the mouth as well;
> Weigh them, it is as heavy; conjure with them,
> DuBois will start a spirit as soon as Garvey.
> Now, in the names of all the Gods at once,
> Upon what meat doth this our Garvey feed,
> That he is grown so great?[7]

In late 1919 or early 1920 UNIA officials, including present and future *Negro World* editors, launched an apparently short-lived journal, the *Weekly Review*. McDonald McLean, its managing editor, was a staunch Garveyite and former editor of a Panama newspaper. Eric D. Walrond was one of the associate editors. He, too, had formerly worked in Panama, as a reporter for the *Star and Herald*. Among the contributing editors were William H. Ferris, Rev. J.W.H. Eason, UNIA chaplain general, and

Professor B.C. Buck, UNIA secretary general.[8] In 1922
Garvey tried to launch a *Blackman* magazine which would
have been devoted to literature as well as to political
affairs.[9] It did not materialize, though he later published
both a newspaper and a magazine bearing that same
name. Had either of these efforts flourished it is likely that
the Garvey Movement's contributions to the arts would
have been better remembered. For historians and literary
critics have hitherto tended to look at magazines (and
mostly the "big name" ones at that), to the exclusion of
the *Negro World*, in their quest for the reality of the
Harlem Renaissance.

The *Negro World* also utilized the common device of
giving away free books with subscriptions to the paper.
Among the books so distributed were J.A. Rogers' *From
Superman to Man*, René Maran's *Batouala* and South
African Solomon Plaatje's *Native Life in South Africa*.[10]

Garvey's periodic International Conventions of the
Negro Peoples of the World also interested themselves in
literary and allied matters. These conventions were
massive affairs. Between 1920 and 1924 they took place in
Harlem and each lasted for the entire month of August.
Delegates came from all over Garvey's far flung domain.
The first, in 1920, is still unsurpassed in the history of
Afro-American conventions. Some 25,000 people from all
over the world filled New York's Madison Square Garden
to overflowing for the opening celebration.

A *Negro World* editorial of April 1922 suggested that
the forthcoming convention should consider com-
missioning a Black scholar to write a comprehensive
history of Black literature. The editorial writer, possibly
Ferris, felt that both Benjamin Brawley's *The Negro in Art
and Literature* and James Weldon Johnson's *The Book of
American Negro Poetry* were defective. Now, he thought,

was "the psychological moment" for such a work, given the burgeoning interest in the subject.[11] This suggestion seems to have come to naught. The convention did, however, appoint a committee on the writing of Black history which suggested that the UNIA should itself reprint and distribute two nineteenth century classics - Robert Benjamin Lewis' *Light and Truth* and the Rev. Rufus L. Perry's *The Cushite*. The committee also suggested approaching Daniel Murray, whose monumental *Murray's Historical and Biographical Encyclopedia of the Colored Race Throughout the World* still remained unpublished after years of effort.[12] They wanted to help him publish it. The UNIA Publishing House, significantly enough, had been established just about three months before the convention.[13] It published UNIA materials, including the two volume *Philosophy and Opinions of Marcus Garvey*.

Women writers and artists were given special encouragement at these conventions. Women's Day at the 1921 convention featured exhibits on art, music, antiques, needle work and literature.[14]

Perhaps the most striking evidence of rank and file literary activity came from the existence of literary clubs in many UNIA branches around the world. Two of the *Negro World's* most prolific poets, J.R. Ralph Casimir of Dominica, West Indies and Charles H. Este of Montreal, Canada, were leaders of their respective UNIA literary clubs. These clubs were following very much in the tradition, already noted, of Garvey's initial UNIA branch in Kingston, Jamaica. They arranged concerts and poetical readings, staged plays and held debates, often against non-UNIA literary clubs and debating societies.

Literary clubs and similar activity were reported also from UNIA branches in Boston, Portland (Oregon),

Santiago (Cuba), Norfolk and Newport News (Virginia), Philadelphia and New York, among other places.[15]

The lack of recognition of the UNIA role in the era of the Harlem Renaissance is again made strange by the fact that the leading *Negro World* literary figures were very much a part of the wider Harlem literary community. Despite their often sharp ideological differences with the integrationist writers and the propaganda debate, there was a surprising amount of interaction among writers of differing persuasions. Perhaps this was inevitable for Harlem, after all, was not a geographically extensive area.

Furthermore, *Negro World* editors and columnists had sometimes belonged to the same organizations as non-UNIA writers in pre-Garvey days. William H. Ferris and John Edward Bruce had both been signatories to the call for W.E.B. DuBois' Niagara Movement back in 1905. DuBois in turn was a corresponding member of Bruce's Negro Society for Historical Research founded in Yonkers, New York in 1911.[16]

Robert T. Browne, a *Negro World* associate editor in the early 1920s and editor in 1933, had been president of the Negro Library Association of New York City, founded in October 1914. Its officers in 1917 included Bruce, Arthur A. Schomburg and Daniel Murray, together with A. Granville Dill, long time business manager of DuBois' *Crisis* and James Weldon Johnson of the NAACP. The Negro Library Association "aimed to collect books, acquire a library building, establish a professorship of Black history and literature, establish an endowment commission, set up libraries in several cities and publish books and a magazine."[17]

The American Negro Academy also provided a forum for the meeting of Garveyite and non-Garveyite intellectuals. It was founded by Alexander Crummell in 1897 to foster Black publications and generally raise the standard of Black intellectual activity. The academy was Afro-America's most select scholarly grouping. The presence within it of several Garveyites and Garvey sympathizers emphasizes the fallacy of the now hopefully discredited view of the UNIA as a movement lacking in intellectual substance.

In so far as it is possible to pinpoint any ideologically identifiable groupings within the American Negro Academy, the Garveyite bloc may well have been the most influential by the 1920s. It included Ferris, Bruce, A.H. Maloney and Robert T. Browne. Arthur A. Schomburg, president of the academy in the 1920s, was a frequent contributor to the *Negro World* and a supporter of Garvey against the DuBois/NAACP camp.[18]

Garveyites who did not belong to the academy also supplemented the work of Ferris, Bruce and company at its meetings. At the July 1920 meeting in New York Ferris read a paper on "The Negro in Prehistoric Times." Bruce read one entitled "Martin R. Delany, An Appreciation." Henrietta Vinton Davis, at various times international organizer and fourth assistant president general of the UNIA, also addressed the meeting.[19] For the academy's 1922 meeting in Washington, D.C., Dusé Mohamed Ali delivered a paper on "The Necessity for a Chair of Negro History in the Universities of the World."[20] This had also been a pet project of Schomburg, of Bruce's Negro Society for Historical Research (of which Schomburg was secretary) and of the Negro Library Association of New York City (of which, as has been seen, both Schomburg and Bruce were members).

Ali was the African who had employed Garvey on his *Africa Times and Orient Review* in 1913. Now he was working for Garvey, as foreign affairs specialist for the *Negro World*. An effort was made to have Garvey himself address the 1922 meeting, but this apparently did not come to pass, perhaps because of Garvey's arrest for mail fraud at about the same time that the meeting was slated to take place.[21]

At the other extreme, W.E.B. DuBois, an early president of the academy and fellow NAACP employees William Pickens and James Weldon Johnson were also members. DuBois and Pickens were leaders of the "Marcus Garvey Must Go" campaign.[22] Perhaps the ideological tensions between these camps may have contributed to the academy's demise in 1928.

The Garveyite artists were equally a part of the literary clubs, lecture series and gatherings of artists that characterized the Harlem of the 1920s. The 135th Street Harlem branch of the New York Public Library (now the Schomburg Center for Research in Black Culture) served as a focal point for much of this activity, through its "Book Lover's Club" and occasional lectures and exhibitions. The Garveyite intellectuals provided a large pool of speakers for the Book Lovers' regular meetings. Ferris addressed them in 1921 on "Negro Prose Writers." E.V. Plummer, a *Negro World* columnist, spoke in 1922 on "The New Negro Seeks Racial Unity." A month later, Hubert H. Harrison addressed the subject of "Books and How to Read Them." Harrison was followed, days later, by Robert W. Bagnall of the NAACP, a leader of the "Marcus Garvey Must Go" campaign and a man who, in 1923, described Garvey as "A Jamaican Negro of unmixed stock, fat and sleek with protruding jaws, and heavy jowls, small bright pig-like eyes and rather bulldog-like face. Boastful, egotistic, tyrannical, intolerant, cunning, shifty, smooth and suave, avaricious...."[23] In 1924 Ulysses S. Poston, UNIA minister of industries and sometime associate editor of the *Negro World*, addressed the book lovers on "Nordic Culture and the Negro."[24]

In December 1922 Carl Van Doren, literary editor of
Century Magazine and a Columbia University professor,
spoke at the 135th Street library. A minor *Who's Who* of
the Harlem literati turned out to hear him, among them
Augustus Granville Dill of the *Crisis*, George W. Harris,
editor of the *New York News* and poet Countee Cullen. A
strong contingent of Garvey editors was there too, including T. Thomas Fortune (then editing Garvey's *Daily
Negro Times*), William H. Ferris and Eric D. Walrond.[25]
For the Garveyite editors it may have been an un-
comfortable experience being in the same audience as
Harris, who was yet another of the "Marcus Garvey Must
Go" campaigners. But the cause of literature and
scholarship continually brought the two camps together.

The 135th Street library also served as the venue in 1923
for a young writers' evening at which Countee Cullen,
Gwendolyn Bennett, Langston Hughes, Sadie Peterson
and Augusta Savage (whose Garveyite connections will be
discussed later) all read their poems. Eric D. Walrond
read a short story. Arthur A. Schomburg and 135th
Street's white branch librarian, Ernestine Rose, were also
present.[26]

This frequent Garveyite use of the library did not deter
the *Negro World* from delivering a sharp editorial rebuke
to Rose when she seemed to step out of line in 1922. The
occasion was her article on "Books and the Color Line,"
published in *Survey* magazine. The *Negro World* explained what the problem was - "Miss Rose writes with
the condescension of the Southerner. In speaking of the
patrons of the 135th street branch of the library, the
taxpayers who maintain it, she describes them as 'black
and yellow, stately Hindoo, proud West Indian, mulatto
American, little black pickaninny, turbanned mammy,
porter, college professor, nurse maid, student.' " The

editorial writer, in all his years as a frequenter of the
library, had never seen a "little black pickaninny" or a
"turbanned mammy" there. He wondered whether "in
her desire to be poetical and picturesque" Miss Rose was
not telling lies. Rose claimed, in defense, that she was in
no way southern. "No doubt," she pleaded, "what you
took to be condescension was merely a mistaken desire to
be picturesque." Her explanation satisfied the paper.[27]

Negro World figures were also active in and around
Harlem's Eclectic Club. Led by William Service Bell,
whom Claude McKay described as "a cultivated artistic
New England Negro," the Eclectic Club was a highly
regarded artistic grouping, judging from the persons who
addressed it. Eric D. Walrond and *Negro World* poet
Lester Taylor were among its members. In January 1922
Dusé Mohamed Ali addressed the club at the Jackson
School of Music at West 138th Street. His topic was
"Modern Egypt."[28]

Claude McKay read selections from his then forthcoming *Harlem Shadows* for the club on April 8, 1922.
Bell supplemented his reading with a talk on Black poetry.
Those present included Arthur A. Schomburg, Zora Neale
Hurston, J.A. Rogers and Sadie Peterson.[29] McKay
recalled later that the club members turned up well
dressed to hear him. He, however, did not own a dress suit
and was apparently the only casually dressed person
present. This did not go down well with those present,
who thought that McKay had deliberately set out to offend
them.[30]

There were, of course, several other salons, clubs and
other venues which served as gathering places for
Harlem's artistic figures. The UNIA hoped that its Phyllis
[sic] Wheatley Hotel would become "one of the literary
forums and social centers of Harlem."[31]

Eric Walrond has left a vivid description of one of these literary meeting places, a tea-shop ("The White Peacock") on 135th Street, near the UNIA headquarters. There, against a backdrop of "futurist paintings" and exotic furnishings, assembled nightly the "musicians and flappers, students and professional people, who sit until far into the night talking about love and death, sculpture and literature, socialism and psychoanalysis.... Harlem's Greenwich Village!" [32]

And just as visitors to Harlem flocked in their thousands to the UNIA offices in the hope of getting a glimpse of Garvey, so too literary visitors were attracted to the UNIA and *Negro World* offices. Fenton Johnson, who had published the unknown Garvey in 1917, was among the 1920 visitors. [33] In 1922 a white writer, Gertrude Sanborn, visited the *Negro World* editors. She had finished *Veiled Aristocrats*, a work on the light-skinned element, for publishers Boni and Liveright (later Walrond's publishers also.) Walrond, Ferris and J.A. Rogers took her to lunch at the Odds and Ends Tea Room at 145 W. 131st Street. [34]

If the *Negro World* editors could join their adversaries at library functions and take a white author to lunch, they could also be quite unselfish in their attitude to other literary efforts in general, and even to those of their adversaries. In 1920 the paper welcomed the new *Upreach Magazine*, published by Willis N. Huggins, M.A., a young Chicago scholar. [35] Huggins later became a leading Harlemite intellectual and a Garveyite.

Ferris even included DuBois in his 1922 listing of the "Twelve Greatest Negroes" - persons who had "made the deepest dent in Negro life and thought and in the life and thought of the world." The full list included Professor William S. Scarborough, Greek scholar; Dr. Francis I. Grimké, theologian; Hon. Archibald H. Grimké, author, diplomat and race leader; W.E.B. DuBois, author and founder of the Niagara Movement; Professor Kelly Miller, mathematician and sociologist; Henry O. Tanner, painter; William Monroe Trotter, agitator; Bishop Levi J. Coppin, biblical scholar and author; Dusé Mohamed Ali, editor of the *Africa and Orient Review* (a successor of the *Africa Times and Orient Review*); Robert T. Browne (of the *Negro World*), author of the *Mystery of Space*; and Marcus Garvey founder of the UNIA, "the greatest living organization." [36]

The *Negro World* was generally favorable to *Opportunity*, the contemporary magazine which, together with the *Crisis*, has received most treatment from historians and literary commentators. [37]

Despite occasional favorable references to DuBois, the paper was less apt to be kind, either to the *Crisis* editor or to his journal. Even here, though, criticisms of DuBois as literary figure were not nearly as harsh as criticisms of DuBois as political activist. In 1922, when the *Crisis* circulation had already begun to decline from its 1919-20 peak, a *Negro World* editorial, "The Passing of the Old Guard," contrasted Garvey and DuBois in terms unflattering to the latter -

> Through Marcus Garvey the Negro youth speaks out. Out on the hilltops his voice is heard. In DuBois, the leader of the old guard, is centered all the ripeness of old age, culture, skepticism, intellectual paralysis. Witness, as exhibit one, the decadence of 'The Crisis,' once a palatable sheet, now a dry, dusty, old-fashioned vehicle of statistics, almost as senile as the 'Amsterdam News.'' [38]

Negro World editors on occasion accused DuBois of egotism, selfishness, duplicity and even plagiarism. Ferris in 1921 documented a devastating list of DuBois' tendencies to plagiarism. He had called William Monroe Trotter a fanatic, only later to produce imitations of

Trotter's *Guardian* newspaper and National Equal Rights
League; his short history of the Negro was nothing but an
abridged version of a longer work by an author he had
previously scoffed at; and he had responded
discouragingly to Dusé Mohamed Ali's plans for a Pan-
African magazine, only to plagiarize Ali's idea.[39]
Historians Carter G. Woodson and Arthur A. Schomburg
both made similar accusations against DuBois from the
pages of the *Negro World*.[40]

Ferris also accused the NAACP generally of ignoring
the "literary, psychic, musical and artistic achievement of
men and women of color who are not in its fold...." The
occasion for this accusation was a 1922 NAACP press
release on Black authors recently published in leading
white magazines. They had ignored an Eric Walrond
article in the *New Republic*.[41] Hubert H. Harrison
similarly complained of having sent DuBois several
hundred copies of Solomon Plaatje's *Native Life in South
Africa* to no avail. DuBois refused to publicize the work.[42]
Plaatje was a founder of the South African Native National
Congress (later African National Congress) in 1912.

Practically all writers on the Harlem Renaissance have
stressed the major role of the literary contests sponsored
by the *Crisis* and *Opportunity* magazines for a few years
beginning in the mid-1920s. James Weldon Johnson
considered them a "decided impulse to the literary
movement" of the period.[43] Yet in this as in so many
other areas, the *Negro World* was earlier in the field - four
years earlier.

The *Negro World* Christmas literary competition of 1921
was a grandiose affair. No less than thirty-six cash prizes
were offered in several categories. These included poetry
(Christmas-related) and essays and short stories on such
topics as "How to Unite the West Indian and American
Negroes;" "The Policy of the Hon. Marcus Garvey;"

"The Negro Problem;" "Aims and Objects of the
Universal Negro Improvement Association;" and "Africa
Redeemed." Apart from the poetry section, the contest
categories all reflected the close ties between art and
struggle in the UNIA. The winning essays were clearly
expected to help solve racial and organizational problems
and reaffirm the goal of African redemption in addition to
being technically meritorious. Yet the judges (Garvey,
Ferris and Bruce) insisted on literary excellence and would
not accept a favorable political perspective as a substitute,
by itself, for good craftmanship. Garvey, judging the
"Africa Redeemed" section, even declined to award a
third prize because, he said, only two entries were well
enough written to deserve prizes. He wrote -

> Among the many papers submitted, I have picked two
> (2) as being meritorious. The others are lacking in literary
> style and proper construction. The authors ought to be
> more careful in their writing, especially knowing that
> awards for prizes can only be given on the general merit of
> the papers submitted. [44]

Winning contest entries were all published in the *Negro
World's* bumper Christmas number. One entrant, a Rev.
C. Anthony Lindsay, won two prizes. The major find of the
contest, however, if later success in the mainstream of the
Harlem Renaissance can be used as a yardstick, was Eric
D. Walrond. Walrond had immigrated to the United States
by way of British Guiana, Barbados and Panama. His
short story, "A Senator's Memoirs," received first prize
from Garvey in the "Africa Redeemed" category. Always
on the lookout for Black talent in any field, Garvey supplemented Walrond's cash prize of $100.00 with a job
offer. Walrond became "assistant to the editor" and then
associate editor. He remained with the paper until 1923. [45]

Walrond, as already noted, emerged in time as the only

important *Negro World* voice against propaganda in art. Yet his prize-winning story on this occasion was a straight-forward propaganda piece, built around the reminiscences of a Congolese senator in a future Republic of Africa. The senator mused over Africa's vast advance during a brief twenty years of freedom. A vast army, a Black Star Line shipping company, a prosperous economy - these were some of the achievements that the senator could look back upon. And all this had been accomplished in the face of dire predictions of doom from the skeptical and the malicious.[46] The story was well enough written and the message clear. Yet it was flat and structurally unexciting. His descriptions of Africans hovered at times on the brink of naiveté. Yet the effort was good enough to launch Walrond on a successful career as a short story writer.

Walrond later worked for *Opportunity* magazine, where the major financial backer for its initial literary contest was Casper Holstein. Holstein, a wealthy Harlemite (reputedly a numbers king), was in the early 1920s a frequent con-tributor of articles to the *Negro World* and a financial supporter of the Garvey Movement.[47] The *Negro World*, in turn, had actively supported his campaign against the United States occupation of his native Virgin Islands. So *Opportunity's* debt to the *Negro World* included not only the precedent of literary contests, but Eric Walrond and Casper Holstein as well. To this list may be added Zora Neale Hurston, whose *Negro World* connections will be discussed later.

The prize-winning essays, stories and poems did not exhaust the artistic fare presented in the *Negro World* Christmas number of 1921. Also featured were a large number of photographs of beautiful Black women from around the world. This, too, was propaganda in art. "Take Down White Pictures From Your Walls," a 1921 *Negro World* advertisement admonished, "Let Them Echo Your

Racial Aspirations." This particular advertisement was for
Garvey quotations artistically printed on wall cards. But
the 1921 photos served at least one similar purpose - to
provide an alternative to white pin-ups.

The Christmas beauties included Amy Jacques, soon to
be the second Mrs. Garvey. Dr. John Wesley Cromwell,
president emeritus of the American Negro Academy, was
very impressed by the Christmas number in general and
the Black and beautiful women in particular. The whole
thing moved him to great feats of lyrical expression. He
wrote, "*The Negro World* Christmas number is a delight
for which to utter loud and long rejoicings, particularly for
the illustrations depicting beauties of the feminine at-
tractions of all varieties and sections of those 'who wear
the shadowed livery of the burnished sun.' " [48]

There can be no doubt but that the UNIA, and more
particularly the *Negro World*, was, in addition to all its
other functions, a major stimulator of literary appreciation. William H. Ferris self-consciously addressed
this fact in an editorial of 1922. He wrote - "While the
Negro World is the organ of the Universal Negro
Improvement Association and hence in some sense a
propaganda paper, we endeavor also to make it a real
newspaper and a literary forum." [49] Nowhere was it more
successful than in its poetical work.

4

Poetry for the People

There exists no greater demonstration of the massive interest in poetry of which Black communities are capable, than that to be found within the pages of the *Negro World*. The Black Arts Movement of the 1960s certainly rivals the poetic interest of the Garvey heyday. But in one crucial area at least, the Garvey era clearly outdistanced the 1960s. For the poetical outpourings of the *Negro World* were thoroughly international, to a degree unmatched by the Black Arts Movement.

The writing of poetry was little short of an obsession with Garveyites. Everybody did it. Rank and file members of the organization did it. The editors and columnists of the *Negro World* did it. Highranking UNIA officials did it. Garvey did it. In addition, sympathetic non-members of the UNIA, some of them important political and literary figures, joined the rush to publish in the *Negro World*.

Poetry was a regular feature of the *Negro World* for practically all of its existence, from 1918 to 1933. The greatest number of poems appeared in 1920 and 1921, most of them part of the "Poetry for the People" section of the newspaper. "Poetry for the People" began in 1920 as a part of the "Magazine Page of the Negro World." It soon gobbled up the rest of the magazine page, and for over a year monopolized a whole page (occasionally more) each week. In 1922 the title "Poetry for the People" was retired. Thenceforth poems appeared on the revived "Magazine Page" and scattered throughout the paper.

So popular had "Poetry for the People" become by 1921

that a single twelve page issue of the *Negro World* once
devoted three pages to no less than twenty-two poems.
And even the large number of published poems
represented but a fraction of those submitted. Editor
Ferris stated that for the January 14, 1922 issue, fifty-five
letters, articles and poems appeared, selected from over
one hundred and fifty submissions from readers.[1]

Ferris from 1920 to 1923 presided with loving care over
the people's poetry. Charles H. D. Este, a prolific *Negro
World* poet and head of the Montreal UNIA's literary club,
spoke for many when he penned the following appreciation to Ferris in 1921 - "I feel it my privilege to
commend you highly on the warm interest and whole-
souled tolerance which you have manifested in the
budding poets of the Negro race. An insignificant aspirant
in the domain of Negro versification myself, I owe you a
lifetime of gratitude for the prominence given me from
time to time."[2]

Este emerged six months later as winner for poetry in
the *Negro World's* 1921 literary competition. Now it was
Ferris' turn, as chief poetry judge, to praise Este, whose
entry he found to be "a jewel of purest ray serene. Its
lightness of spirit, simplicity of style, beauty of imagery
and rhythm of verse," he said, "made it a real poem."[3]
Este's poem was given a whole page in large type.

Negro World poets came from everywhere - the United
States, Canada, the U.S. Canal Zone (Panama), Jamaica,
Dominica, Cuba, Barbados, Grenada, Guatemala,
Venezuela, Brazil, Sudan, Mexico, Nigeria, the Gold
Coast (Ghana), British Honduras (Belize), Colombia,
Liberia, Bermuda and more. They wrote mostly in
English, though the paper's Spanish section sometimes
carried poems in Spanish as well.

Theirs for the most part was fighting poetry, the poetry

of an oppressed people who would be free. It is here, in
the pages of the *Negro World*, that anyone must look who
would discover the real artistic voice of the rank and file
New Negro. They wrote of love and flowers and sunsets to
be sure, but overwhelmingly they wrote of the struggle to
be free, of death to the Ku Klux Klan, of an Africa
redeemed, of repatriation to the Motherland, of the
fighting spirit of the New Negro, of their organization, the
Universal Negro Improvement Association, of their
leader, the Honorable Marcus Mosiah Garvey. The
question of art versus propaganda exercised the minds of
few *Negro World* poets, even though the paper's editors
struggled with it. The Vietnamese leader, Ho Chi Minh
(himself an admirer of Garvey), would have approved of
their work, for it was Ho who penned these lines -

> The men of old times like to write about nature.
> Rivers. Mountains. Mists. Snow. Flowers. Moon. Wind.
> We must arm the poetry of our days with steel.
> And our poets must learn to fight battles.[4]

A sampling of *Negro World* poetic titles presents a
poignant collage of the UNIA's ideological images -
"Lord, Lift Our Race;" "A Call to Race Manhood;" "The
Message of Freedom;" "Four Million Strong;" "When
Africa Awakes;" "On, On to Abyssinia;" "Oh,
Motherland!" "Reflections of a Slave;" "Africa Is
Calling;" "The Black Star Line;" "Ye Sons of Ham;"
"Africa! Africa! My Own Beloved Land;" "One God, One
Aim, One Destiny [the UNIA motto];" "Battle Hymm of
Ethiopia;" "Call of the UNIA;" "Elegy Written in a
Strange Land;" "Let The Black Man Cross the Sea;" "Ku
Klux Klan Beware!" "The New Negro Woman's Attitude
Toward the White Man;" "Marshal the Sons of Africa."

Perhaps the single most popular subject for the *Negro
World* poets was Marcus Garvey. A sampling of the

paeans in praise of their leader makes an equally eloquent
collage of the esteem in which he was held - "Lines to His
Excellency Marcus Garvey;" "A Tribute to the Hon.
Marcus Garvey;" "Words of Condolence to Marcus
Garvey;" "Garvey's Fame;" "Homage to Garvey;" "Our
Leader's Prayer;" "He Came By Way of New Orleans;"
"Can We Forget Marcus Garvey?" "Tell It Out;"
"Something New Under the Sun;" "O Praise the King of
Glory;" "Acrostic on Marcus Garvey;" "Marcus Garvey
Our Moses;" "Sonnet to Hon. Marcus Garvey;" "Marcus
and I;" "Garvey's Accomplishments."

Leaders have been immortalized in verse since time
immemorial.   Toussaint L'Ouverture received com-
mendatory attention from William Wordsworth and John
Greenleaf Whittier. But few must be the modern leaders
upon whom have been heaped the volume of poetical
adulation that Marcus Garvey received.

Negro World poets, as a group, therefore, differed in
their choice of subject from the better-known "mainstream" poets of the Harlem Renaissance. It was not that
their range of subject matter was so different. But they
were much more likely to write unambiguously racially
committed poetry. Stylistically, however, there were more
similarities. Many of the *Negro World* poets, like their
better-known contemporaries, strove to emulate the
poetical masters of earlier eras. They produced what
Claude McKay called "Verses... written in the style of
Pope, Dryden, Goldsmith and Longfellow...." [5] There
were shades of Phillis Wheatley everywhere. Some attempted what Frank Harris, editor of *Pearson's Magazine*,
thought he saw in McKay's own work, namely a "classical
feeling and a modern way of expressing it." [6] A small
number tried avant garde prose poems, in at least one
case with conspicuous success. Like their better-known
contemporaries, they turned their backs on Afro-American

dialect poetry despite a general fondness for Paul Laurence Dunbar. Indeed, the absence of such dialect verse was more nearly total among the *Negro World* group than among the white-published group. Such fiercely race-conscious men and women were unlikely to use a form so steeped in connotations of white condescension and Black belittlement. The only *Negro World* regular to devote any significant attention to dialect verse happended also to be the paper's only white poet (of whom more anon). There also appeared at least one rare attempt at West Indian dialect. Parodies of well-known poetical standards appeared from time to time. The trenchant "With Apologies to Shakespeare," already noted, was one of the best examples of this genre.

A noteworthy aspect of the "Poetry for the People" columns is that they often contained, side by side with the poems, articles on questions of poetics. These were usually written by the poets themselves, though Ferris and other *Negro World* staffers sometimes joined the discussions. These aspiring poets showed great familiarity with the history of Western poetical writing. A correspondent from El Callao, Venezuela, writing on "What Is Poetry?" (a standard caption for these articles on poetics), quoted Latin poetry in Latin.[7]

The UNIA regularly honored historical personalities by naming ships, school buildings, and the like after them. Booker T. Washington, the educator, politician and author, and Phillis Wheatley the poet were the most frequently so honored. Washington had a ship and a school named after him. The Black Star Line paid a substantial downpayment on, but never did acquire, the *S.S. Phyllis Wheatley* ("Phyllis" being the more common, though technically incorrect spelling). This was intended to be the line's most important vessel and was earmarked

for the New York/West Indies/Liberia route.[8] The Phyllis
Wheatley Hotel shared premises with the Booker T.
Washington University at 3-13 West 136th Street in
Harlem. It had accommodations for one hundred and
thirty guests and was officially opened on July 31, 1922.[9]

Both Washington and Wheatley appear at first sight to
be strange UNIA heroes. Washington is often seen as an
Uncle Tom figure. But Garvey preferred to see in him his
positive qualitites of self-reliance, race pride and Pan-
African consciousness.[10] The situation is similar in
respect to Wheatley. Modern critics have traditionally
seen her as mostly devoid of racial commitment, but this
view can admit of some modification.

The majority of Wheatley's poetry obviously dealt with
non-racial themes and there were good reasons for this.
For one thing, she was snatched from her native African
land at the tender age of seven or thereabouts. Thereafter
she lived in what, for a slave, was a most atypically
privileged environment. She never knew the rigors of
plantation life. Instead she experienced, and was to some
degree accepted into, the genteel life of rich and cultured
white New Englanders. In addition, many of her poems
were written on commission. This explains the large
number of funerary odes among her surviving works.
Those who commissioned her work were white. Furthermore, the surviving poems of Phillis Wheatley are far
from a complete record of her work. Perhaps among her
lost poems there may have been more on the subject of her
Africanness in the midst of a white world. She also died at
the young age of about thirty, at a time when her perspective on the world may not have been fully developed.
After all is said and done, however, the fact remains that
Phillis Wheatley was not entirely insensitive to the racial
question. Given her situation, the fact that she wrote any

race poetry at all has to be seen as a positive fact in itself. Many of her references to Africa, slavery and the like occur in unexpected places, in poems that ostensibly have nothing to do with racial questions. (One wonders if those who have commented on her even took the time to read all her surviving work). In verses "To His Honour The Lieutenant-Governor, on the Death of His Lady, March 24, 1773," for example, she refers to herself as "the Afric muse."[11]

In "To The Right Honorable William, Earl of Dartmouth, His Majesty's Secretary of State for North America," Wheatley makes the interesting point that she, as a victim of slavery, can well appreciate why the North American colonies would desire freedom from England -

> I, young in life, by seeming cruel fate
> Was snatched from Afric's fancy'd happy seat:
> What pangs excruciating must molest,
> What sorrows labour in my parent's breast!
> Steel'd was the soul and by no misery mov'd
> That from a father seiz'd his babe belov'd.
> Such, such my case. And can I then but pray
> Others may never feel tyrannic sway?[12]

Even Wheatley's best known, seemingly reactionary lines can be interpreted in a less negative ((if not positive) light. In "On Being Brought From Africa to America" she said,

> Twas mercy brought me from my Pagan land,
>   Taught my benighted soul to understand
>   That there's a God, that there's a Saviour too
> Once I redemption neither sought nor knew.
> Some view our sable race with scornful eye;
> 'Their colour is a diabolic dye.'
> Remember, Christians, Negroes, black as Cain,
> May be refined, and join the angelic train.[13]

Wheatley was here denouncing racial prejudice in the only
way that her experience would allow - within the narrow
confines of a conservative Christian indoctrination.
Persons with much more radical reputations, such as the
great Pan-African, Bishop Henry McNeal Turner, accepted the same basic assumptions about the redemptive
value of Christianization. Turner, of course, went much
further than Wheatley. He saw Western education as well
as the Gospel as part of the redemptive value of slavery.
And he wanted the African to take whatever he had ob-
tained in the West and run back home with it. Turner said
in 1895, "I believe the Negro was brought to this country
in the providence of God to a heaven permitted if not a
divine-sanctioned manual laboring school, that he might
have direct contact with the mightiest race that ever trod
the face of the globe."[14]

The point simply is that Phillis Wheatley has to be seen
in her own context, and in that setting she was not as bad
as may appear at first sight. And whatever her politics,
she did strike a blow for African intellectual capacity at a
time when Thomas Jefferson thought the race incapable of
comprehending Euclid, and quite possibly the offspring of
orangoutangs.[15]

The most prolific of the *Negro World* poets was, like
Phillis Wheatley, a woman. She was Ethel Trew Dunlap, a
UNIA member, first of Chicago and later of Los Angeles.
Week after week she poured forth a torrent of poetic
commentary on the vicissitudes of being Black in white
North America; on the hope provided by Marcus Garvey
and the UNIA; on her personal experience of the racial
problem; on the stirrings of African peoples internationally. The *Negro World* described her in 1922 as a
"California poetess whose verses have brought bushels of
inspiration to Africa's sons and daughters in their fight for

complete emancipation."[16]

Dunlap displayed some poetic talent and in a different place and time may have achieved more lasting acclaim. She knew very well, though, what it meant to be an uncompromisingly racially committed Black poet in the United States of the Garvey era. It meant dedication and sacrifice and little hope of the material rewards that an equal effort would command in other situations. She addressed this reality in "Black Bards" (1921). She wrote,

> Poets who are seeking for a wreath,
>   If your ancestors are of dark descent,
> Consider, ere you dip your pen in ink
>   Or to the muse your earnest ear is lent,
> The obstacles that you will meet ahead,
>   The entrances that will be closed to you;
> The exits that will furnish no egress
>   Where progress points the bard he must go through.
> Consider criticism's searching eyes
>   That turn the X-ray on the trembling soul;
> Consider all the stately ships that pass
>   The frailer bark bound for success's goal.
> And worse the silence which thou must endure
>   Until hope droops her weary, lagging wing,
> And jaded thoughts all hollow-eyes surround
>   Thy soul aspiring that had hoped to sing,
> And then, dark bard, if thou canst patient be -
>   If it will not be to thy soul distress,
> While others wear the laurels, to confine
>   Thine appetite to flavor of success -
> Dip pen in ink and loose the prisoned thoughts
>   That shall go forth to set a nation free -
> Burn evil's rubbish piles with virtue's torch -
>   And thou indeed a noble bard shall be![17]

Dunlap's sentiments here are reminiscent of the later and better known concluding lines of Countee Cullen's "Yet Do I Marvel"-

> Yet do I marvel at this curious thing:
> To make a poet black, and bid him sing! [18]

"Black Bards" did not exhaust the list of problems facing Black poets. Dunlap poignantly catalogued some more of these in "Good Bye, Black Belt" (1921), subtitled "Lines written just before leaving Chicago for Danville, Illinois, en route to Los Angeles, California" -

> Black Belt, you cannot nurse a rose,
>   And poets long for flowers.
> I've tried to hide it and be brave,
>   But, oh, I long for bowers...
> Some twilight that is all serene,
>   Where Ephraim and I
> Forget the White Curse when we gaze
>   Into God's starry sky.

But her despair was only fleeting, for she concluded,

> So farewell, Black Belt, for a while;
>   But if I hear you groan,
> Back on the wings of love I'll fly
>   To dusky, barren zone. [19]

Dunlap's reference to Ephraim was one that was repeated in many of her poems. She explained that Ephraim was "a creature of my imagination," a personification of "The Ethiopian... race," based on biblical references (Genesis, 46:20 and Hosea, 5:14) to the son of Joseph who departed from the true faith and later returned to God. [20] She was not the first to use Ephraim this way. [21]

Like the traditional *griots* of West Africa and the calypsonians of the Caribbean, the *Negro World* poets faithfully recorded and commented upon the racially significant events of the day. Dunlap's "The Tulsa Race

Riot'' (1921) lent poetic supplement to the anguished
chorus that rose from the Black community -

> O Tulsa! while my pen wrote on
>   And fancy rode through Paradise,
> From out thy smold'ring, crumbling ruins
>   Rose Egypt's sons' and daughters' sighs.
> The strong have smote the weak again,
>   And thou must bear the curse of Cain! [22]

In "The Peonage Horror" (1921) she bitterly lamented
yet another southern outrage, this time the much
publicized mass murder of Black peons by white farmer
John S. Williams in Jasper County, Georgia. There was
almost a Tennyson-like pastoral quality about this poem,
which rendered it strangely, beautifully incongruous for
the ghastly deed she set herself to chronicle. A deep
feeling of melancholy suffused the work and left the
reader in a state of numbness beyond the reach of immediate anger -

> Where the Yellow River murmurs there's a hush -
> Even day dawn wears a guilty tell-tale blush -
>   And the waves are icy cold
>   At the horrors that unfold,
> Where they sweep through Jasper County with a rush....
>
> Breezes, that brush by the river's winding shore,
> Murmur supplications that are heard no more -
>   Whirlpools gurgle like the breath
>   Of the victims sent to death -
> Where the slave trade thrives as in the days of yore.
>
> Where the earth is trembling to give up its dead -
> Where the peon dug his yawning, awful bed,
>   There's a deathlike silence there,
>   Poisoned is the very air,
> Where the blood of Abel has been sought and shed.

Even spring has lost the gayness of its bloom,
And its blossoms feel the coldness of the tomb,
    Where the pit and where the wave
    Yield the unwilling grave
For the victims peonage sent to their doom.

Where the red man wandered by the rippling wave
Of the Yellow River, while his soul grew brave,
    Where fond lovers row at eve -
    Lilies bloom - white doves grieve -
Lurks the phantom spirit of the outraged slave.

Winds in Jasper County sigh the awful tale -
Captives' groans are mingled with their nightly wail,
    Where they went to ghastly death,
    Robbed of God's most precious breath,
Where the Yellow River leaves its silver trail. [23]

Ethel Trew Dunlap also wrote several poems to Marcus
Garvey, with titles such as "Sail for Garvey's Goal"
(1921), "In Respect to Hon. Marcus Garvey" (1922) and
"In Respect to Marcus Garvey" (1921). The following
stanza from the last mentioned is typical -

He saw a flag eyes could not see -
    A nation yet unborn -
A land where black men might be free,
    The dawn of freedom's morn. [24]

Dunlap's poetry covered a range of subjects almost as
wide as that of all the other *Negro World* poets put
together. In "On, On To Abyssinia" (1921) she espoused
the Garveyite goal of repatriation -

On, On to Abyssinia!
    Why should we tarry here,
Where we are tossed about like chaff
    And chased like routed deer? [25]

Her "Onlys" (Onliest?) of 1922 provided a unique affirmation of the enduring qualities of "Black English." In a way it presaged the debate on this question that was to intensify a half century later -

> I'll teach you English, how to cast
>   Aside your Negro dialect;
> But there's a word I hesitate,
>   In spite of grammar, to reject;
> 'Tis onlys. Ephraim, of course,
>   You never knew you spoke it so.
> It sounds peculiarly sweet -
>   And so, I think, I'll let it go.[26]

Ethel Trew Dunlap was a very light hued individual, though her commitment to Garvey's program was not lessened thereby. She made a conscious decision to identify with the African side of her mixed ancestry. She confessed to her extended family of *Negro World* fellow poets,

> I am not black as Kedar's tents and yet
> There is a tie that binds to Afric son
> And daughter that enthralls me and enchants -
> So count me thou as Ethiopian.[27]

This question of her skin color caused Dunlap considerable pain in her private life. But so secure did she feel in her *Negro World* community of poets that she was willing to bare her soul to them. In "If I Should Die Tonight" (1922), she produced a lovely, melancholy, introspective, almost self-pitying cry of anguish at her dilemma as a light-skinned champion of the African race -

> If I should die tonight, perchance
>   Someone who is born fair
> Might gaze into my face and see

> The lines of sorrow there,
> And whisper: "She was freedom's child;
>   She loved the outcast slave."
> And those who chided me in life
>   Might pity by my grave....[28]

"If I Should Die Tonight" was a cry for help, perhaps written in a moment of depression. Help was forthcoming almost immediately. H.A. Nurse of Winnipeg, Canada, responded with "If You Should Die Tonight - To Miss Ethel Trew Dunlap" (1922) -

> If you should die tonight
>   And never more should sing,
> The sun's ethereal light
>   No joy to me would bring;
> 'Twould be a sorry world,
>   How could I deem it right
> If God should claim your soul
>   Before you've won your fight?....[29]

Dunlap was a favorite with the community of *Negro World* poets - and they were indeed a community. They criticized one another's work, dedicated verses to one another and on occasion carried on extensive conversations via their poetic offerings. Dunlap welcomed and encouraged these exchanges. "Write to me, O sons and daughters / Of a race that is oppressed, " she proclaimed in "To The Sons and Daughters of Ethiopia" (1923). One who apparently did write her privately was sixteen year old Geneva Williams, whose letter to the *Negro World* had not been published. Dunlap consoled her in "Lines to 16 Year-old Geneva Williams" (1921) -

> We cannot print your letter, dear -
>   The paper lacks the space;
> But Marcus Garvey's working hard

To free your outraged race....

Several poets addressed lines "To Miss Ethel Trew
Dunlap," to which she dutifully responded in kind. In this
practice, the poets for the people were simply being heirs
to an ancient tradition. Jupiter Hammon, Afro-America's
first poet, had directed similar lines to Afro-America's
second, in "An Address to Miss Phillis Wheatley,
Ethiopian Poetess, in Boston, who came from Africa at
eight years of age, and soon became acquainted with the
Gospel of Jesus Christ" (1778).[30]

Dunlap was also the subject of some literary criticism. A
correspondent from Cayo Mambi, Cuba, well nigh
overreached himself in his florid exuberance. He wrote,
"As the artist portrays the [ga?]laxy of the butterflies as
they frolic among the busy bees o'er the flowers of a
beautiful orchard overshadowed by the sunbeams of a
tropical sun, twinkling o'er the horizons of time, so it is
that Miss Dunlap in her poems unfolds the beauty of
creation, the riches of Africa and the philosophy of
humanity. On the whole she dwells on the faithfulness of
Garvey and the possibility of his achievement." He
thought her a "modern Phillis Wheatley."[31]

Fellow poet Marion S. Lakey sympathetically pinpointed
a technical weakness in Dunlap's work. "Miss Dunlap,"
he observed, "seems to have but one notable handicap in
writing her poetry. She seems to lack the power of
carrying in her poems a large amount of intricately
arranged rhyme without apparent difficulty." He was
aware that "this seeming handicap will count little if any
against her in the popular view" but cautioned that it
would loom large if she was to entertain hopes for critical
success.[32]

Another "Poetry for the People" regular was Leonard I.
Brathwaite of New York. He was, like Dunlap, a poet of

some promise. His style, however, was very different. Brathwaite produced poetry that was beautiful in an unconventional kind of way. His avant-garde prose poems prefigured, to some extent, some of the Black Arts Movement poetry of the 1960s.

Occasionally, his prose poems would break into semi-conventional verse. Sometimes they would go to the other extreme, with long paragraphs of apparently straight prose. The overall effect of his poems was often that of an embryonic short story, complete with plot and, usually, stating some moral. Among the better-known Harlem Renaissance poets, Fenton Johnson's prose poems came closest to Brathwaite's. But whereas Johnson's sarcasm sometimes gave way to deep and unrelenting despair, Brathwaite more typically preferred the devices of humor, satire, and sarcasm too, to make his point.

Brathwaite's "In Covington, Georgia" (1921), dealt with the same event as Dunlap's "The Peonage Horror" -

> Somewhere out
> * * *
> In Covington, Ga.,
> * * *
> A white planter
> * * *
> And his Negro foreman
> * * *
> Are held for
> * * *
> The killing of
> * * *
> Eleven Negro 'peons.'
> * * *
> They are alleged
> * * *
> To have been killed

* * *
By the Negro foreman
* * *
At the instigation
* * *
Of the white planter.
* * *
The Negro Foreman:
* * *
He cannot read,
* * *
He cannot write,
* * *
He does not know
* * *
From where he came
* * *
But
* * *
He remembers himself
* * *
Living in
* * *
Jasper County.
* * *
This Negro,
* * *
Attributes
* * *
The following statement
* * *
To his 'Master,'
* * *
Mr. Johnny:
* * *
'It's either
* * *
Their necks
* * *
Or your neck.'
* * *
And when

* * *
The curtain
* * *
Will have been
* * *
Let down
* * *
On this
* * *
Most horrid
* * *
Of dramas
* * *
I wonder
* * *
What
* * *
Will be
* * *
The attitude
* * *
Of the American public
* * *
North and South,
* * *
East and West,
* * *
Towards the Negro
* * *
As their 'civilization'
* * *
Affects him.
* * *[33]

Brathwaite's moralizing was even more clearly stated in "Big Negroes" (1921) -

The "Big Negro,"

* * *
Is he really big?
* * *
The "Little Negro,"
* * *
Must he stay little?
* * *
It would be well
* * *
For all concerned
* * *
If the would-be
* * *
Big Negroes
* * *
In the process
* * *
From little to Big
* * *
Brighten their intellect
* * *
And curb their egos
* * *
And get real big
* * *
And "broad";
* * *
Help and co-operate
* * *
With the little Negroes....[34]

In "Poise" (1922) Brathwaite's visual presentation was a little more conventional, but the general feel of the poem was the same -

There is the individual who, when one approaches
Tries to seem dignified, owlish, cultured and learned;
And when one gets close to him, if his head he has turned,
He's sure to seem spasmed; then contracts and gives a smile,
As if he were a Colossus and one looked up at him awhile....[35]

Brathwaite also contributed several letters to the *Negro World*. In one he urged Black people to master science and technology. In another he provided a harsh review of Lothrop Stoddard's *The Rising Tide of Color Against White World-Supremacy*.[36]

Charles H. D. Este published regularly, both before and after his success in the 1921 literary competition. "To Marcus Garvey" (1921) was somewhat different from the usual Garvey praise songs. It never mentioned Garvey by name (except in the title). Instead he painted an allegorical picture of his journey through a dark and friendless night -

> The night was cold the wind was high;
>   The path I trod was rough and drear.
> No voice I heard; no friend was nigh,
>   My mind was filled with doubt and fear....

In the midst of his fright and despair an apparition (Garvey) presented itself and pointed the way, no doubt to personal as well as group salvation -

> I looked across the pasture wild,
>   And there I saw you robed in white.
> 'Gird up your loins little child,'
>   The voice replied in language bright.
>
> At this the night grew calm and bright.
>   A yellow light illumined the way;
> And all the shades of gloom and fright
>   In sudden rush were chased away.[37]

The *Negro World* regulars did not write a great deal of non-political poetry. But some such did appear. Ernest E. Mair contributed one, "To My Antidote," in 1922 -

> Oh, it is wonderful to have a friend

> Who understands your mood,
> Where gentle pressure of the hand
> Uplifts you when you brood.[38]

Mair grew up in the Jamaican parish of St. Ann, Garvey's birthplace. His "The Green Hills of Saint Ann" (1923) is reminiscent of Claude McKay's "Flame Heart" and other nostalgic poems and stories of home. The remembrance of an idealized St. Ann was for Mair a "home of refuge" from the rigors of a transplanted North American existence -

> A place brimful of memories
>   Of my childhood days gone by,
> Where prone upon my back beneath
>   Its glorious skies I'd lie.
> A desired home of refuge
>   To a travel-wearied man
> Is my old home town that nestled
>   On the green hills of St. Ann.[39]

When Mair did turn his talents to political poetry, it was with a vehemence that again recalls the spirit of McKay's "If We Must Die." In a long poem, "Hypocrisy" (1922), Mair lashed out at England for its racist objections to the presence of French African troops of occupation on the Rhine. He reminded England of its initial refusal to allow West Indian and other colonial troops to participate in its "white man's war" of 1914-1918. As the war progressed and England faced the stark possibility of defeat, expediency triumphed over sentiment -

> His boastful words of yesterday -
> "This is a white man's war" -
> Were dropped, and in the race to die
> Down went the color bar!

Now that the war was over the German, the depraved Hun of British wartime propaganda, became a creature worthy of salvation from contact with African troops. Mair predicted a violent and ignominious end to this empire built on oppression -

> O England! queen of hypocrites,
> That wields the cruel rod
> Which bleeds the Ethiopian's back,
> Prepare to answer God!
> For though his mills grind slowly,
> They grind exceeding small;
> Your kingdom built on blood and tears
> Is rushing to its fall.[40]

One of the most prolific *Negro World* poets of all was J.R. Ralph Casimir of Dominica, West Indies. He headed the local UNIA and belonged to its literary club. In addition to poems, he also contributed articles on political conditions in Dominica and the activities of his UNIA division. Occasionally, he wrote under the pseudonym "Civis Africanus" (Citizen of Africa). Casimir's poems ran the gamut of poetical subject matter. Typical titles were "Dominica and Her Afric Sons;" "Hats Off to Bellegarde" (an acrostic inspired by a speech to the League of Nations by Dantes Bellegarde, Haitian representative to that body); "On to Africa;" "Battling Siki" (in honor of the African boxer's knockout defeat of French and European champion, Georges Carpentier); "Haiti, Awake!" "Under the Bamboo Tree;" "Paul Laurence Dunbar;" and "My Books." Casimir once tried his hand at West Indian dialect in "Sal's Sweeties" (1922).

Some of his poems were praise songs to *Negro World* editors and UNIA officials. One such, "O Loving Sage," (1923), was dedicated to Ferris -

O Loving Sage of a noble race,
I'm glad to note that you embrace
Wisdom so charmingly,
Giving light to mine and me....[41]

In 1946 Casimir published, in a Garveyite journal,
"Marcus Garvey - Dead." This was six years after Garvey's death and is an eloquent tribute to the man's life and
work -

Persecuted by white folk
    And cheated by his own,
He fought for Afric's welfare
    To cowardice not prone....

Bow down in shame ye traitors
    Who tampered with his plan,
What plan have you to offer
    To help the African?[42]

Casimir maintained contact with other race journals,
both Garveyite and non-Garveyite, from around the world.
After the *Negro World* was banned by the British
colonialists in West Africa he regularly mailed copies to
J.E. Casely Hayford, the Gold Coast (Ghana) Pan-
Africanist and editor of the *Gold Coast Leader*. [43] One of
Casimir's poems, "To the Africans at Home," appeared
in the *Gold Coast Leader* in 1922. [44] The *Negro World* was
banned in some West Indian territories too, but Dominica
was not one of them.

Casimir published several volumes of verse over the
years. Several contain reprints of his *Negro World* poems.
Among these works are *Poesy: An Anthology of Dominica
Verse* (1948), *The Negro Speaks* (1969), *Farewell (and
Other Poems)* (1971) and *Black Man, Listen! and Other
Poems* (1978).

At least three *Negro World* poets are among the figures

usually considered important, if not major, Harlem
Renaissance personalities. In the case of none of them are
their Garveyite connections known (or acknowledged).
The three in question are Lucian B. Watkins, Augusta
Savage and Zora Neale Hurston.

Sergeant Lucian B. Watkins was born in Virginia and a
veteran of World War I. The war cost him his health and
he died in a hospital at Fort Henry, Maryland on February
1, 1921, four days before his last poem appeared in
"Poetry for the People." Indeed, he had been practically a
weekly contributor to this page during the last year of his
life.[45]

Watkins' last *Negro World* poem, "Loved and Lost"
(1921) was a most poignant swan song, heavily laced with
a premonition of impending death. He wrote,

> My fallen star has spent its light
>   And left but memory to me;
> My day of dream has kissed the night.
>   Farewell; its sun no more I see;
> My summer bloomed for winter's frost;
>   Alas, I've lived and loved and lost!

Watkins was greatly mourned by the confraternity of
Negro World poets, several of whom composed memorial
verses. Thomas Millard Henry penned "A Sonnet In
Memory of Lucian B. Watkins" (1921) -

> What is so sad as when a poet dies
> Whose song was sweet and bold, whose face was black,
> Whose audience had not evolved, alack!
> To cherish all he brought them from the skies?....
> He sang and "loved and lost," but nevermore
> Will such sad themes be his; for at the gate
> Of sweet Elysium he'll learn a song
> With raptures deeper than was his before....

Robert T. Kerlin, a well-known white compiler of an
anthology of Black poetry, joined his efforts to the *Negro
World* panegyrists. He too, like Henry, commented upon
Watkins' last poem. "No one can read his last poem," he
wrote, "which has the proverbial sweetness of the dying
swan's song, without saying to himself, 'A genius is
bidding a sad, sweet farewell to earth.' "[46]

Contributing editor Hubert H. Harrison used Watkins'
death to emphasize a point he had made before, namely
that "our Negro poets never get properly noticed by us
until they have been taken up either by death or by the
white people."[47]

William H. Ferris eulogized Watkins by way of an entire
editorial. "He was one of our contributors," Ferris wrote,
"who we could rely upon to give us real poetry. The poems
and sonnets were full of thought, delicate in sentiment,
graceful in form, and rythmical." Ferris quoted a lengthy
portion of Watkins' 1920 contribution to the ongoing
"Poetry for the People" dialogue on "What is Poetry."
Watkins had written -

> The writer believes that poetry has a spiritual
> significance that is essential towards the evolution of
> human souls. Poetry is the Music of the deep, the Har-
> mony of the height, the Law of the Universe. It was born
> when "In the beginning God created the heaven and the
> earth." It breathed when, "the spirit of God moved upon
> the face of the waters." It spoke when "God said let there
> be light, and there was light." Poetry paints with the
> colors of immortal imagery, sings with the melodious
> word-notes of pulsing gladness, talks in Hallowed
> Parables. Only the ordained seers, peers and apostles
> appreciate it in the fullness of its God-given glory. It seems
> that its picture need not always be beautiful; it may even
> be admirably awful, its story need not always be true, it
> may be an exquisite exaggeration, a magnificent lie. Its

song need not always be reasonable, it may be beneath,
above or beyond reason. Its charm is subtle as life itself.
We love it for its joy, yet may cherish it in spite of its pain.
We are drawn to it as the bird is helpless before the
bewitching eye of the serpent.

Poetry is a bit of God's Kingdom "On earth as it is in
Heaven." It soothes and sustains life in its restless
longings for the unattainable. It is the heartbeat of
humanity, the march step of life, the wheel of time, the
ceaseless cycle of existence.

> One with its beauty and its song
>   We dream its dream - eternal whole;
> As o'er the lines we linger long
>   Its spirit breathes in each soul.

Ferris loved this essay. "Perhaps," he mused, "the
brave poet achieved immortality in that article. Some
literary critic may come along and regard it among the
world's classic descriptions of poetry."[48]

James Weldon Johnson included three of Watkins'
poems in *The Book of American Negro Poetry* (1922). In
Alain Locke's 1925 anthology on *The New Negro*, both
Locke himself and William Stanley Braithwaite described
him as a major poet.

Augusta Savage is best known as a sculptor, but she
also achieved some recognition as a portrait artist and a
poet. A native of Florida, she moved to Harlem in 1921 to
pursue studies in sculpture at Cooper Union. In 1922 Eric
Walrond published an interview with the twenty-one year
old Savage in the *Negro World*. Accompanying
photographs showed her together with her bust of Marcus
Garvey. She had also completed a bust of W.E.B. DuBois,
at the request of Sadie Peterson, librarian and poet. The
DuBois bust was shortly to be presented to the 135th
Street library.[49]

By 1923 the *Negro World* was carrying advertisements

for Savage's Garvey busts, life size as well as smaller.
"Critics declare," the blurb read, "that these busts are
the true likeness of the Hon. Marcus Garvey. They are
done in bronze and are the work of a young Negro
sculptress."[50]

Savage was later to gain national acclaim, but in the
1920s acceptance across the color line was not always
easy. On May 5, 1923 the *Negro World* editorially scored a
"committee of famous artists" for denying Savage a study
trip to France on racial grounds. "Miss Savage shows
promise as an artist," said the *Negro World*. "Her friends
were ready and willing to defray all of the expenses of the
trip. But the committee of American artists thought her
dusky hue might raise the race question."

Augusta Savage moved among the mainstream of
Harlem's literati. In 1926 she joined Zora Neale Hurston,
Langston Hughes, Wallace Thurman and others in the
production of the important but short-lived *Fire!!*
magazine. She also contributed poetry to the *Negro
World*. Her "Supplication" (1922) was built around the
Lord's Prayer -

> Our Father, great and good Jehovah,
>   Whose own Son to mortals came,
> And whom saints adore in Heaven,
>   Hallowed be thy name....[51]

"The Old Homestead" (1922) was a nostalgic
remembrance of her Florida home, similar in feel and
spirit to Ernest E. Mair's "The Green Hills of St. Ann."
Harlem was a land of immigrants, and such nostalgia was
inevitable -

> I visited today the old Homestead,
>   Deserted now for many busy years,

Explored again with memory laden tread,
   The birthplace of so many hopes and fears.

The windlass seemed to creak a doleful tune,
   The mocking birds that used to sing so gay
Seem all forgetful of the month of June,
   The time to sing their merriest roundelay.

The meadow that to childish eyes did seem
   To stretch into the distance mile on mile,
Is but a glen, and now the raging stream,
   Is just a little brook that tries to smile....

And down my time scarred cheek there crept a tear,
   For those who sleep beneath the ocean's foam,
And then a sigh for other hearts so dear,
   That rest so gently 'neath the sand of home.[52]

Savage's melancholy here was sadly anticipatory of a
great calamity that would ere long befall both her and the
UNIA. For her husband of all too brief a time was soon, as
it were, to "sleep beneath the ocean's foam."

Augusta Savage cemented her ties to the Garvey
Movement when she married one of the UNIA's brightest
and most promising young leaders, Robert Lincoln Poston.
Poston was born in Hopkinsville, Kentucky, in 1890. His
father was an instructor at the State Normal School at
Frankfort, Kentucky and his mother was a county school
supervisor. Poston attended Walden University in Nashville, transferring at the end of his third year to Howard
University. From Howard he moved to Boston for
elocution lessons. His next move was back to Hopkinsville,
where he taught school for several years.

Poston enlisted at the onset of World War I and was
promoted to sergeant in three days. Within a month he
was recommended for a commission; but a hostile encounter with a white sergeant suddenly brought him face

to face with the prospect of incarceration. He was forced, as he put it, "to wage one of the greatest legal battles undertaken by any colored person" during the war. Poston was eventually reduced in rank but was nevertheless honorably discharged eleven months later. He did not see service overseas.

On his return to Hopkinsville, Poston published the *Hopkinsville Contender*, but it was not long before racism embroiled him in its tentacles once more. He protested the fact that Black veterans were relegated to the back of a local victory parade and was accordingly prevented from publishing his paper. So he moved it to Nashville. This proved too expensive, so he and his brother, Ulysses, emigrated to Detroit, where after a few months they began publication of the *Detroit Contender*. Within eight months the new paper had surpassed all its local rivals in circulation.

It was about this time that Marcus Garvey came to town. The Poston brothers heard him speak and were won over immediately. They joined the Detroit UNIA. Robert L. Poston afterwards attended Garvey's Second International Convention of the Negro Peoples of the World in New York in 1921. Here he attracted Garvey's attention. A New Negro, young and fearless, well-educated and articulate, he was the kind of person that Garvey could not allow to slip by. Garvey nominated him for the post of second assistant secretary general of the UNIA. Poston was elected. Thereafter his rise in the association was rapid. He immediately became a regular contributor to, and editorial writer for the *Negro World*.

In 1922 Poston became secretary general of the UNIA and in August of that year he received the UNIA decoration of Knight Commander of the Order of the Nile.[53] His brother, Ulysses S. Poston, meanwhile ex-

perienced an equally rapid rise within the organization. By
1922 Ulysses was the UNIA's minister of industries and an
associate editor of the *Negro World*.

In December 1923 Robert L. Poston travelled to Liberia
as head of a UNIA delegation for talks with that country's
government. This was to be his last service to the UNIA,
for he died tragically on the way back. The cause of death
was pneumonia and it happened at sea on March 16, 1924,
just twenty-four hours out of New York.[54]

Poston's death was a great loss to the UNIA. In addition
to all his other duties he had just been named secretary of
the Black Cross Navigation and Trading Company, successor to the organization's Black Star Line Steamship
Corporation. The *Negro World* carried a front page eulogy
by Marcus Garvey. "We say farewell to Robert Lincoln
Poston," Garvey declared, "but not good-bye, for he is
still with us. We see him every minute; his picture cannot
escape us. We see the man still serving us. We see his
spirit moving. We know that Poston's soul is so fixed that
he is omnipresent in the cause of the Universal Negro
Improvement Association and African redemption. We
know that wheresoever Poston is at this hour, if the soul
can act and think then he is acting, working and thinking
for the cause for which he died and which he loved so
much. Let us pray for the repose of his soul, yea, pray that
that soul will have immediate entry into heaven and there
forever rest in peace."[55]

As a mark of final respect the UNIA elevated Poston to
the rank of prince, its highest honor. His body lay in state
overnight at Liberty Hall, guarded by members of the
Universal African Legions, the organization's paramilitary
force. From there it was placed on a train to Hopkinsville,
escorted by a UNIA funeral party. The *Negro World*
commented, "It was the funeral of a Prince. Ethiopia has

stretched forth her hands unto God, and a Prince has already come out of Egypt!"[56]

Poston's death was but the first half of a double tragedy for Augusta Savage. She retired to her Florida home to await the birth of their child. The baby, Roberta L. Poston, was born on July 21, 1924 but died shortly thereafter.[57]

Several of Poston's *Negro World* articles had been on literary and artistic subjects. He was also, like his wife, a *Negro World* poet. One of his early poems, a patriotic work entitled "I'll Be Back," was published during the war in *Trench and Camp Magazine* and "was circulated extensively among the soldiers."[58] His *Negro World* poem, "When You Meet A Member of the Ku Klux Klan" (1921) was a militant example of the New Negro spirit -

> When you meet a member of the Ku Klux Klan,
> Walk right up and hit him like a natural man;
> Take no thought of babies he may have at home,
> Sympathy's defamed when used upon his dome....
> Call your wife and baby out to see you have some fun,
> Sic your bulldog on him for to see the rascal run.
> Head him off before he gets ten paces from your door,
> Take a bat of sturdy oak and knock him down once more.
> This time you may leave him where he wallows in the sand,
> A spent and humble member of the Ku Klux Klan. [59]

Zora Neale Hurston is another of the luminaries of the Harlem Renaissance who benefitted from early exposure in the *Negro World*, a fact of which her biographer is totally unaware.[60] Indeed, the *Negro World* seems to have provided her with her first large-scale national and international exposure. Prior to the *Negro World*, she had published in campus publications at Howard University.[61]

Hurston's *Negro World* work consisted of poems, short sketches of life in Harlem and a short account of a visit to Arthur A. Schomburg's library in Brooklyn.[62] Contrary to

her biographer's opinion, she seems already to have made
her entree into Harlem's literary circles at this time
(1922). Her visit to Schomburg's library was in the
company of Eric Walrond of the *Negro World* and others,[63]
and she attended Claude McKay's reading before the
Eclectic Club of Harlem.[64]

Her first *Negro World* poem was called "Night" (1922)
and consisted of four lines -

> When night opens her shining eyes,
>   And spreads her velvet gown;
> She softly paints the purple skies
>   In grays of cloudy down.[65]

She followed with "Journey's End" (1922), apparently an
attempt at an auto-epitaph -

> Ah! let me rest, when I have done,
> Beneath a warming, stirring sun,
> Beneath a flower-studded sod
> That shows the smiling face of God....
>
> Ah! let me rest when I have done,
> When I my earthly course have run,
> And wake me not to shame or blame,
> Nor stir my dust with flore of fame.[66]

A third poem, "Passion" (1922), looked back over her
short life with a sense of self-satisfied finality, strange for
one barely into her twenties. "I could die happy," she
seemed to say, "for I have lived and loved" -

> When I look back
> On days already lived
> I am content.
>
> For I have laughed

With the dew of morn,
The calm of night;
With the dawn of youth
And spring's bright days....

And I have loved
With quivering arms that
Clung, and throbbing breast -
With all the white-hot blood
Of mating's flaming urge.[67]

Unlike most of her fellow *Negro World* poets, Zora
Neale Hurston's submissions were entirely lacking in any
political content. She obviously had not entered into that
spirit of Garveyism which fairly exuded from the works of
so many of the others. Hurston was a bright young woman
on the way up and she did not mind using whoever
happened conveniently to be in a position to be used. A
succession of wealthy and influential sponsors would soon
help her on her way and at that point she would be quite
happy to burn the Garveyite bridge she had crossed.

This she did in 1924 in a scurrilous story entitled "The
Emperor Effaces Himself."[68] It was intended for
publication and she sent a copy to Carl Van Vechten. She
began with a description of Garvey's 1924 convention
parade which, for all its flippant humor, still provides
some useful details of this spectacle -

Eight modest, unassuming brass bands blared away
down Lenox Avenue. It was August 1, 1924, and the
Emperor Marcus Garvey was sneaking down the Avenue
in terrible dread lest he attract attention to himself. He
succeeded nobly, for scarcely fifty thousand persons saw
his parade file past trying to hide itself behind numerous
banners of red, black and green.

This self-effacement was typical of Mr. Garvey and his

organization. He would have no fuss nor bluster - a few thousand pennants strung across the street overhead, eight or nine bands, a regiment or two, a few floats, a dozen or so of titled officials and he was ready for his annual parade.

As the article progressed the satire became more vicious. Hurston accused Garvey of fraud and poked fun at his very reasonable campaign to have African peoples portray God in their own color. She seemed to have visited Garvey's apartment, or at least to have received a description of it from someone who had. "On the walls of his living room in 129th Street," she declared, "there hung a large picture of Napoleon. On the opposite wall hung one, still larger, of himself. It is evident he wished no comparisons drawn. If he had, he would have caused them to be hung side by side."

People like Hurston (and Walrond, as we will see) reflected the price that the artists of the Harlem Renaissance too often had to pay for entry into the mainstream of white acceptance. They had, as it were, to ritualistically renounce their Garveyite connections as a sort of condition precedent to acceptance into the respectable world of major publishing houses. One could be a Garveyite and settle down for a struggle to win recognition the hard way - the way that Ethel Trew Dunlap had chosen. This way was not impossible but it was hard. Or one could renounce one's Garveyite past and hope for quicker recognition, provided one had the talent and the connections. This way was not easy. But it was easier than the hard way.

Nor were the likes of Zora Neale Hurston guessing when they thought that the Carl Van Vechtens of this world would expect anti-Garveyism from their Harlem protégés. In his *Nigger Heaven*, Van Vechten clearly indicated what their attitude to Garvey should be - "I might open a beauty parlour," said one of his characters, Mary. "Yes, you might," came the rejoinder, "but there are forty of those on every street in Harlem already. And you might start another Black Star Line, or peddle snow...." Elsewhere in the book Van Vechten thusly ends a discussion on the merits and demerits of racial solidarity - "Bottle it, Dick, said Olive. You'd think this was a Marcus Garvey meeting...."[69]

In the 1940s and '50s another generation of artists had to face a similar dilemma, this time in reference to communism. Richard Wright, like Hurston, renounced his early support, this time from the Communist Party. Paul Robeson refused unequivocally to disavow his ambiguous flirtations with communism, and suffered.

Savage, Watkins and Hurston were not the only *Negro World* poets to achieve significant attention. Some of them were, or became, well-known political figures. One such was T. Albert Marryshow of Grenada, a man remembered in the history books as the "Father of West Indian Federation." Marryshow was for several decades a leading nationalist politician in Grenada and the Caribbean. In 1920 he contributed a political poem, "And Yet!"-

> Poor rags and all tatters
>   My portion might be,
> And yet robbed in Manhood
>   No slave dwells in me;
> The world's dearest mantle
>   Is true liberty![70]

From the Gold Coast (Ghana) came several poems by the important West African nationalist and Garvey admirer, Kobina Sekyi. Sekyi, a lawyer, held the degrees of B.A. and LL.B. and was, as the *Negro World* put it, "one

of the few" persons "who has been able to apply Western
intellectual influence to African needs." In the 1940s he
exerted significant influence over Kwame Nkrumah,
himself a Garvey admirer and later first leader of independent modern Ghana. Sekyi's poems were published
through the good offices of Dusé Mohamed Ali, Effendi.[71]
Sekyi's "The Sojourner" (1922) was one of the two longest
poems ever published in the *Negro World*. The other was
Garvey's "The Tragedy of White Injustice" (1927).

"The Sojourner" is divided into four sections -
"Untravelled," "Abroad," "Retrospective" and "Home
Again (To Africa)." It is an epic of an African's journey
from innocence to assimilation to rude awakening and
back to grateful rediscovery of his heritage. It was a poetic
reflection of Sekyi's own journey from Africa to England
and back. It began in the first person, with the brainwashed African expressing contempt for his unassimilated
brothers -

> A product of the law school, embroidered
>   by the high,
> Upbrought and trained by similar products,
>   here am I!
> I speak English to soften my harsher
>   native tongue,
> It matters not if often I speak the
>   Fanti wrong.
> I'm learning to be British, and treat
>   with due contempt
> The worship of the Febich, from which
>   I am exempt.
> I was baptized an infant, a Christian
>   hedged around,
> With prayer from the moment my being
>   was unbound,
> I'm clad in coat and trousers, with
>   boots upon my feet,
> And tamfuraga and Hausas I seldom

> deign to greet;
> For I despise the native that wears the
> native dress,
> The badge that marks the bushman who
> never will progress....
> I soon shall go to England, where I've been
> often told,
> No filth and nothing nasty you ever
> may behold,
> And there I'll try my hardest to
> learn the English life,
> And I shall try to marry a real
> English wife!

Arrived in England, the African is shocked by the inhospitable climate, the capitalistic greed and the contradiction of technological progress co-existing, uncaring, with abject misery. He would fain return home. Only his desire for the white man's education prevents him from quitting this strange land. He exclaims,

> Deep Poverty ranged by the side of
> wealth,
> Is that what thou would'st call Civilization?

This shocking encounter with England brings reflection and reactive self-realization. History moves in cycles. Europe did not always rule the world. Africa has nothing to be ashamed of. The time has come for Africa to bestir herself -

> Awake thee from thy slumber
> And quickly disencumber
> Thy manhood of the fetters
> That make thine equals betters.

The African who returns home after such an English ordeal is not the brainwashed would-be Afro-Saxon who left, but a new African, full of love of self. He vows undying love for his country. He is prepared to look with compassion even upon her faults -

> Thou hast thy faults, but some are tender faults:
>   Thy freeness with thy trust,
> Hath laid thee open to the base assaults
> Of foreigners. Thine openness exalts
> In needless gifts, that but increase their lust.[72]

Sekyi's poem was as good an example as any of the Garveyite ideology which most *Negro World* poets exhibited. In some ways "The Sojourner" also presaged the Negritude movement of the 1930s, whose African and Caribbean poets fell back upon a love (sometimes even an exaggerated love) of their own, as a reaction to European cultural imperialism.

An important, though little known, influence on the New Negro movement was George Wells Parker, founder of the Hamitic League of the World. Parker was a graduate student at Creighton University in Omaha, Nebraska and developed a reputation, especially among Black nationalist circles , for his expertise in ancient African history. His 1918 publication, *Children of the Sun* (published by the Hamitic League of the World at 933 N. 27th Street in Omaha),[73] utilized the testimony of ancient Greek and other writers in support of Africa's claim to be the cradle of civilization.

No less an authority than J.A. Rogers has acknowledged his indebtedness to Parker. Rogers wrote, "From two works by Negroes I received much perspective and valuable leads. These were George Wells Parker's *Children of the Sun* and William H. Ferris' two-volume work, *The African Abroad.*"[74] Parker was much in demand as a speaker in the Chicago area and Rogers, a some time Chicago resident, may have met him there, as did Harry Haywood, later a well-known Afro-American communist.[75]

Parker was deeply impressed by Garvey.[76] His poem,

"When Africa Awakes!" appeared in the *Negro World* in
1923. Its affinities with Garvey's own ideas were apparent-

> Africa bides her time! But from the ocean strand,
> O'er jungle, mountain, vale and mead,
> That sweet word, "Unity!" will speed
> On Wings of winds, and woo her fretful folk
> Into one dream, one voice, one heart, one hope!
> And yet again she'll claim her sacred right
> To rule herself, apart from alien might;
> But if, once more, the pale-faced men shall say:
> "Not Yet, thou backward race! Still thine to pay!
> I quake to think how swarthy arms shall hurl
> Thundering terrors at a gasping world!
> When Africa awakes![77]

Parker is thought to have died young.[78]

The *Negro World* editors themselves exhibited a strong
tendency towards poetical writing. Almost without exception they combined wide-ranging literary and artistic
appreciation with their political, journalistic and broader
intellectual pursuits. In 1921, about two years before he
became its editor, T. Thomas Fortune's "The Black Man's
Burden" appeared in the *Negro World*. It was a parody of
the notorious "White Man's Burden" by Rudyard
Kipling, the "poet laureate of British imperialism."
Fortune's poem began -

> What is the Black Man's Burden,
> Ye hypocrites and vile,
> Ye whited sepulchres
> From th' Amazon to the Nile?
> What is the Black Man's Burden,
> Ye Gentile parasites,
> Who crush and rob your brother
> Of his manhood and his rights?

Fortune's dislike of Kipling was every bit as virulent as
that of H.G. Mudgal, previously quoted. Mudgal was

John Edward Bruce and
Dusé Mohamed Ali, Effendi

The UNIA Dramatic Club, 1921

UNIA Women, 1921, including Amy Jacques, Soon-to-be Wife No.2

William H. Ferris

himself a *Negro World* editor after Fortune's death. His
poetry appeared in 1922 and for many years thereafter.
Hubert H. Harrison, Robert Lincoln Poston and John
Edward Bruce were among the editors who also were not
loath to break into occasional verse. Marcus Garvey, as
managing editor, can be included here.

The venerable Bruce, old enough to be Garvey's father,
published a short poem, "Success"(1922) which he
dedicated "To Marcus Garvey" -

> Would you count it and wear its bright token?
>   Smile and step out to the drummer's light lilt?
> Fight on till the last inch of sword blade is broken?
>   Then do not say "die" - fight on with the hilt.

William H. Ferris, the *Negro World's* major poetry
critic, surprisingly did not join his fellow editors and poets
for the people.

Dusé Mohamed Ali, Garvey's former African employer,
edited a foreign affairs section in 1922. But like Fortune
and Mudgal, he made his *Negro World* debut as poet, in
1921. Another of his poems appeared in 1922.

Women were well represented among the Garveyite
poets. The woman question also provided a popular theme
for these poets, both male and female. Some such poems
were couched in the form of tributes to the Black woman -
tributes to her beauty and her grace. Two 1923 titles by
J.R. Ralph Casimir of Dominica were typical of this genre -
"Negro Women: An Appreciation" and "Love's
Greeting." Part of Garvey's plan included the
rehabilitation of the Black woman's good name from the
negative stereotypes prevalent in the larger society. These
poems were a reflection of that effort, however traditional
and a-political they might seem when viewed out of
context.

Such poems also made the simple statement that "Black
is beautiful." Ernest E. Mair's "O Afric Maid" (1922) was

a charming example -

> O Afric maid whose beauteous eyes,
>   Whose voice, whose smile I idolize
> Whose name enchantment spells for me
>   O Afric maid, I dare love thee!

Ethel Trew Dunlap's similarly entitled "Sweet Afric Maid" (1922) weaved a similar message around biblical characters -

> Sweet Afric maid, sweet Afric maid!
> Be my Zipporah, fond and true.
> As Moses fled to Midian,
> A fugitive, I come to you.[79]

Sometimes the effort to reclaim the Black woman's good name from hostile stereotypes took a more militant form. "The New Negro Woman's Attitude Toward the White man" (1921) by Estella Matthews was the best example of this -

> Laugh with your lustful eyes,
>   We will never bend our knees.
> The shackles ne'er again shall bind,
>   The arms which now are free.[80]

Ethel Trew Dunlap also addressed herself to the white man's lust. Like the anti-lynching crusader Ida Wells Barnett before her, she attacked the white male rationale for the lynching of Black men - the supposed necessity of keeping actual and potential Black rapists at bay. In "The White Woman Speaks White Woman's Defense" (1922), Dunlap had the white woman seek common cause with the Black man, both victims of a white man who had robbed the Black woman of her honor -

> Clasp hands with me, O Afric son!
> Oppression makes our hearts as one.

> I speak for daughters of the free.
> No longer slaves our sex will be
> To white lords who have ruled with lust
> And trailed the Afric maid through dust....
> Don't hang a black man to a tree
> And try to blame your crime on me.[81]

One of the most imaginative poems on the woman question came from the avant-garde Leonard Brathwaite. His "At the Masked Ball" (1922) addressed itself to an intra-racial problem which manifested itself acutely in the area of male-female relationships -

> She was a beauty in her mask and costume.
>
> Her shapely contour, her agile carriage, lent grace to her make-up.
>
> Her deep, resonant but exceedingly mild voice - a voice heated by the suns of Africa and tempered by the bleak ozone of these United States of America - would have wooed and charmed anyone. She would have made Ponce de Leon exclaim "I've found it!...."
>
> The waltz was through. The ball was over. They had exited to go home. She had removed her mask. "Horrors! She's black. I thought I was dancing with and would have been escorting home a high-yallah![82]

Negro World poets, as has been seen, were male and female, from the New World and the Old, leaders and followers of the Garvey Movement. In J.M. Stuart-Young, however, the *Negro World* had a most unlikely poet. For he was white and English. He was also one of the most persistent of *Negro World* regulars. Most of his poems appeared in 1922 but they were still being published in 1929. Nor was Stuart-Young a poet only. He was also a contributor of prose.

Negro World poets usually avoided Afro-American dialect, but Stuart-Young had no reason to. His "Heart-cry" (1922) sounded like an attempt to imitate Paul Laurence Dunbar -

> Where's ma honey? Where's ma honey?
>   Gone away! Gone away!
> Dearer far than wealth of money,
> With her smile so sweet an' sunny,
>   Gone away! Gone away!....[83]

If Stuart-Young had ever visited the United States, this fact was not mentioned. He was, however, a widely travelled sojourner in tropical lands. His submissions were as likely to originate in Onitsha, Nigeria, as in London. Some were reprints from the *Gold Coast Leader*, a publication sympathetic to Garvey.

Stuart-Young may have endeared himself to *Negro World* readers with articles such as a 1924 one which the paper captioned "White Man Condemns Misrule in Nigeria." On other occasions, though, his perspective was less enlightened and took full advantage of the paper's liberality towards his efforts. J.R. Ralph Casimir of Dominica attacked him in 1922 for suggesting that some Black people were happy under the British flag. Casimir objected also to his reference to "the threatened world climax toward which the extreme Garveyites are leading black thought."[84]

Stuart-Young was a published author and in 1929 he sent the *Negro World* a review of his novel *What Does It Matter?* from the English based magazine, *West Africa*. The story was that of a boy's hard life in Manchester. The *West Africa* reviewer considered it "an astonishing achievement, when one reflects that it has been put together under the terrific sun of Nigeria by a writer who at the same time is earning a livelihood as a business man."[85]

The *Negro World* in 1922 considered compiling an anthology of its verse,[86] but this project sadly was not consummated. Nineteen twenty-two was the year of Garvey's arrest for alleged mail fraud. He was convicted and jailed for good early in 1925 and deported to Jamaica in 1927. These were years of turmoil and trauma for the UNIA, and these events probably pre-empted the time and resources which might otherwise have gone into such a project.

"Poetry for the People" certainly lived up to its name. It enabled large numbers of people to obtain international exposure and it directed poetic energy into socially meaningful channels. Several of the *Negro World* poets adopted as a title for their poems a phrase which aptly summed up their work - "More Truth Than Poetry."

None was more aware of the "truth" of Garveyite poetry than those forces of law and order who waged a protracted struggle against the movement. United States Attorney General, A. Mitchell Palmer, reacted with alarm to the 1919 *Negro World* poem, "This Must Not Be!" by Carita Owens Collins -

> This must not be!
> The time is past when black men,
> Laggard sons of Ham,
> Shall tamely bow and weakly cringe
> In servile manner full of shame....
>
> Demand, come not mock suppliant!
> Demand, and if not given - take!
> Take what is rightfully yours;
> An eye for an eye;
> A soul for soul;
> Strike, black man, strike!
> This shall not be![87]

5

Book Reviews

It may come as a great surprise to many to learn that the *Negro World* prided itself on being the first Afro-American popular publication to carry a regular book review section. The pioneer in this field was Hubert H. Harrison, a *Negro World* editor from 1920 to 1922. Harrison expressly rejected any claim that W.E.B. DuBois' *Crisis* magazine might have to pioneering status in this field - indeed, he viewed his rival's belated competition with disdain. Writing in March 1922 he declared, "It is now two years since I inaugurated in this newspaper the first (and up to now the only) regular book-review section known to Negro newspaperdom. Since that time I have observed that the magazine called *Crisis* has been attempting to follow my footsteps with such success as was achievable by youth and inexperience."[1] The "youth" of Harrison's scornful allusion was probably Jessie Fauset.

By 1922 Harrison was also being challenged by a large corps of able reviewers within the *Negro World* itself. Harrison commented, "I foresee that in the near future there will be many book reviewers... among us. Indeed, they are already treading on my heels in this paper...."[2] The reviewers treading on his heels included Ferris, Bruce, Walrond, Arthur A. Schomburg, J.A. Rogers, Dusé Mohamed Ali and Robert L. Poston. Some letter writers also sent in unsolicited reviews. There was even a most unlikely regular reviewer in Mary White Ovington, who was not only as white in fact as she was in name, but also chairman of the board of directors of the NAACP.

Book reviews and review essays enjoyed wide popular

support and sometimes generated commentary in the
letter-to-the-editor columns. Some popular books were
reviewed several times over by different writers. Reviews,
like other forms of literary expression, even made their
way into the paper's editorial columns. Reviews were still
appearing at the paper's demise in 1933.

Harrison had for long been one of Harlem's most
respected intellectuals. He was born in St. Croix in the
Danish West Indies and toured the world with a yachting
party of young scientists in 1899, before settling in New
York in 1900.[3] He was well-known on the streets of
Harlem as a soap box orator and political activist. For a
time he had been a prominent member of the Socialist
Party but had left it because, as he put it, he preferred
"race first" to "class first."

Harrison's book reviewing career began in 1906 in the
New York Times.[4] He also authored books and published
a magazine, *The Voice*, before joining the editorial staff of
the *Negro World* in January 1920.[5] In 1917 he founded the
Liberty League, which provided the young Marcus Garvey
with one of his earliest important platforms before a
Harlem audience.[6] At his death in 1927, at the age of 44,
he was described as a staff lecturer for the Board of
Education in New York City and a "special lecturer" in
Contemporary Civilization at New York University.[7]

Being a pioneer Black reviewer was not without its
difficulties. Harrison discussed the principal of these in an
article entitled "On A Certain Condescension in White
Publishers." Even though by 1922 many of the major
publishing houses were sending him review copies, some
were still doing so reluctantly. Boni and Liveright (who
later published Eric Walrond) had initially refused to send
him any books at all. All of this, said Harrison, was but a
reflection of an age-old problem - white publishers viewed
the Black market with scorn. "As the only certificated
Negro book-reviewer in captivity," he wrote, "I feel the
onus of this backward view which white publishers take of

the market which the Negro reading-public furnishes for their wares. It is not complimentary to us: it is short-sighted and unsound. After all, pennies are pennies, and books are published to be sold. We believe that the Negro reading public will buy books - when they know of their existence. One sees proof of this in the amazing stream of letters and money orders which flow in to Mr. [J.A.] Rogers at 513 Lenox Avenue for his books, *From Superman to Man* and *As Nature Leads*." [8]

Despite his strong race position on some issues, Harrison's perspective could at times be erratic and unpredictable. On such occasions he would have to contend with problems of a different sort, namely irate letters from *Negro World* readers. The lady from Cambridge, Massachusetts who practically called him an Uncle Tom for his favorable review of Eugene O'Neill's play, *Emperor Jones*, was a good example of this.

Harrison's reviews were only a part of his wider interest in literary criticism. He lectured regularly at the 135th Street library in Harlem on such literary figures as Edgar Allan Poe, Macaulay, Victor Hugo, "Lincoln as a Master of English," Lewis Carroll and James Russell Lowell.

Eric Walrond rivalled Harrison for the number of his reviews. He could be unstinting in his praise, as when he found not a single mediocre poem in Claude McKay's *Harlem Shadows*. [9] Or he could be forthright in his criticism, when he found nothing to praise. On William Pickens' *Vengeance of the Gods* he had this to say - "a book of fiction, or a book masquerading as fiction, ought to at least tell a story, and tell it straight." [10]

Mary White Ovington shared, with the Englishman J.M. Stuart-Young, the distinction of being one of the *Negro World's* two white regulars. Her "Book Chat" column was a fairly regular feature in 1921 and 1922. After a lengthy hiatus beginning in late 1922 it reappeared briefly in 1923. Ovington was chairman of the board of an

organization which was waging war against Garvey. Some
high-ranking NAACP officials were directly involved in
the campaign to have Garvey imprisoned and deported,
even while Ovington's reviews were appearing weekly in
the *Negro World*.[11] Garvey himself seems to have considered her no different from other white NAACP leaders
who were "disarming, dis-visioning, dis-ambitioning and
fooling the Negro to death."[12] Yet he apparently tolerated
her appearance in the *Negro World*.

It may be that Ovington's column was a useful political
ploy. For one thing, she held her fellow board member,
W.E.B. DuBois, in a contempt not too different from
Garvey's.[13] She may also well have been a pre-*Negro
World* acquaintance of one of the paper's editors, perhaps
Ferris or Harrison.[14]

In her "Book Chat" Ovington tried to sound as pro-
Black as she was able. A Southern professor had once
mistaken her novel, *The Shadow*, for that of a Black
writer, she exulted. That had made her very happy.[15]
(Black critic, William Stanley Braithwaite, also had some
nice things to say about *The Shadow*.)[16] Ovington's 1922
review of William Ellery Leonard's *The Lynching Bee and
Other Poems* illustrated well her capacity for righteous
vehemence. Leonard was a white University of Wisconsin
professor, which fact Ovington considered significant.
"And every time a man of this calibre turns upon his own
race," she said, "and shows it in its basest aspect, we
need to note and give thanks."[17]

Ovington tended to review mostly the works of white
authors on race subjects. The other reviewers con-
centrated mainly, though not exclusively, on Black
authors. The two most-reviewed authors of all were René
Maran and J.A. Rogers.

René Maran was born in Martinique in 1888, emigrated
to France at an early age and later found employment as
an official in the French colonial service in Africa. He

became something of an overnight sensation in French and international literary circles when he won the prestigious Goncourt prize for literature in 1921, for his novel *Batouala*. Interest was fed as much by his work as by the fact that he was Black.

Batouala was set in Ubangui-Shari (now the Central African Republic) in French Equatorial Africa. It was a story of adultery, where the villian walked off with the prize, the favorite wife of Batouala, a powerful and popular chief. Maran was an incredibly keen observer of the African environment which he helped administer. He provided vivid insights into the lifestyle, modes of thought and natural surroundings of the people he described. His observations had all the detail of a social scientist, but embellished by the stylistic panache and eloquent language of the master novelist.

An atmosphere of sensuality pervaded the book, resulting in some mild "censorship" in the first United States translation. Maran also utilized the same unemotionally stark realism, alike for what was sordid and for what was beautiful in African life. And always, hovering over the novel, there was the presence of the exploiting white colonialist and the mixture of resentment, awe and derision with which the Africans viewed his intrusion into their land. Only in the preface did Maran seem to side explicitly with the Africans against the European colonizer.

Several of the *Negro World's* big guns reviewed *Batouala*, some in more than one article. Ferris, Walrond, J.A. Rogers, Ovington and Harrison all had their say, as did others, less well-known. Alain Locke, editor of the seminal anthology on *The New Negro*, and a person not normally associated with the Garvey Movement, analyzed *Batouala* at length in a long review article on "The Colonial Literature of France."[18]

There was an enigmatic quality about *Batouala*. Like the

Mona Lisa, who alternately smiles and frowns, depending upon the predisposition of the beholder, Maran's novel seemed propagandist to the propagandists, non-propagandistic to the anti-propagandists and somewhere in between to those who straddled the fence.

Alain Locke, though writing *in* the *Negro World*, was not really *of* the *Negro World*, and so he surprised nobody when he saw in *Batouala* "art for its own sake combined with that stark cult of veracity - the truth, whether it hurts or not, for the sake of eventual peace of human understanding."[19]

The same could be said of Mary White Ovington, despite her strenuous efforts to "relate" to her Garveyite surroundings. Ovington did not await the English translation. She read the book in its original French, a feat equalled by J.A. Rogers. "If we look at 'Batouala' as propaganda for the Negro," she warned, "we shall be sadly disappointed. It depicts a grossly sensuous tribe held in subjection by a brutal government. But as a picture of the horrors of imperialism it has never been surpassed."[20] Ovington's last sentence here contradicted the rest of her passage somewhat and highlighted the Mona Lisa quality of the novel.

Ferris came closest to accepting the enigma as it was, without trying to resolve its apparent contradictions. This was easy for Ferris to do, since it fell right into line with his long-espoused view of propaganda. The best propaganda novel, he had long argued, was the one which weaved its message subtly and understated, into a powerfully told, technically proficient, skillfully executed story. "There is nothing wrong in a propaganda novel or play per se," Ferris wrote. " 'Ben-Hur', 'Uncle Tom's Cabin' and 'The Scarlet Letter' show how powerfully propaganda can be woven into a story."[21]

Batouala was Ferris' kind of novel. It seemed a perfect vindication of the point he had been making for so long.

"And here is where 'Batouala' differs from a propaganda novel per se," he wrote - he seemed almost to rejoice - "although it has a powerful propaganda effect. Rene Maran's ideas of the harshness and severity of French rule in equatorial Africa are not consciously forced upon the reader, but are revealed naturally in the course of the story."[22]

Ferris commented on *Batouala* more than once over a period of several months. His major review, however, came in the form of a very long editorial. Here he made essentially the same point - "we have no quarrel with Mr. Maran because he gave us a work of art instead of a sermon or essay in the guise of a novel....There should be no straining for effect, no overanxiety to preach a sermon, point a moral and teach a lesson. Then the novel, play or poem will bring its message as a novel, play or poem...."[23]

Yet even Ferris could not entirely escape the enigma of *Batouala*. He found Maran's much talked about realism to be wanting. He thought that Maran could have done a little more for the African without transgressing the bounds that Ferris had sketched. "Realistic art is art," Ferris pointed out, "but idealized art is higher art .... Maran is a great artist, a great word painter, but he would be a greater artist if he saw the African not only as he actually is but as it is possible for him to become - the rawstuff and raw material out of which manhood is made."[24]

J.A. Rogers may well have argued that Maran had already done what Ferris was suggesting. For Rogers saw in Batouala nothing less than the prefiguration of a new African man of whom future generations could be proud. Rogers analyzed this point better than any of the other reviewers. He wrote,

Because Rene Maran writes with the calm, close

restraint of the perfect artist, who never sentimentalizes or
holds out an index finger, people have failed to see that for
the main figure of his book he has picked out that rarest of
creatures in modern civilized life, a man. Batouala, the
chieftain, is a man, a sturdy, upright character. Apply the
simple test of justice, honor, courage and he comes
through magnificently, in heroic size.

He was a champion of his people and their customs.
Nothing could make him swerve in this respect. By contrast, Bissibingui, the handsome young wife-thief, was
willing to betray his people and go over to the whites and
help them in their cruel exploitation of the blacks. As for
Batouala, no amount of oppression could make him yield to
the whites in an essential. In non-essentials, where the
welfare of his people was concerned, he would yield..., but
in nothing else. He could not be bent. That Rene Maran
means to show this trait clearly in Batouala comes out in
the end when he says of him: "He fell to the ground un-
bending, as falls a tall, mighty tree."[25]

Rogers' was essentially a pro-propaganda position.
Other reviewers, in more typical *Negro World* style,
expressed this view more forcefully. Hubert H. Harrison
spoke of "Maran's bill of indictment against the bar-
barous brutality of French rule"[26] and G.M. Patterson
saw *Batouala* as "something to awaken the consciousness
of his group everywhere."[27] Walrond seemed curiously
out of step with his fellow reviewers of whatever persuasion when he rather inanely described Maran's novel
as "a series of poetic jungle pictures around which are
built a story of savage dramatic interest"[28] - nice words,
signifying little.

Maran himself, it is only fair to add, contributed his
share to the enigma of *Batouala*. For in his preface he had
simultaneoulsy claimed objectivity for the novel and
explicitly denounced French colonialism.

Batouala was distributed in the United States by a
Harlem company, Minor and Patterson. It was heavily
advertised in the *Negro World* which by November 1922
was offering free copies with subscriptions to the paper.

Maran's work could not help but have influenced the Harlem Renaissance, coming as it did at the beginning of the 1920s. If nothing else it held up an attractive precedent for Black literary success. And Maran in his preface had specifically tied his novel's timeliness to the Afro-American question. "My book is not trying to be controversial," he wrote therein. "It appears, by chance, when its time has come. The Negro question is relevant. Who willed it so? Why, the Americans."[29]

J.A. Rogers (1880-1966) rivalled Maran for the position of most-reviewed *Negro World* author. If Maran's book was more intensely analyzed over a shorter period (mostly during 1922), interest in Rogers' books, and his own involvement with Garvey and the UNIA, were spread over a much longer period.

Rogers, like Garvey a Jamaican by birth, had been acquainted with Garvey since their youth in Jamaica. He interviewed Garvey in London three years before the latter's death in 1940. Rogers' works on little-known aspects of Black history have been classics in the Black community since the World War I period. Lack of interest on the part of white publishers caused Rogers to publish his books himself. Only after his death did one of his works find favor with a major publisher.

During the 1920s and afterwards Rogers worked as a journalist and his articles were carried in many Black publications. His relationship with the *Negro World* and the UNIA was always close.

Rogers first arrested the attention of the reading public with *From Superman to Man* (1917). The book took the form of a dialogue between a racist United States senator from Oklahoma (a man of "pronounced views," according to the dust jacket), and a "polished, well-educated universally-travelled" Black porter on a trans-continental train. The porter, Dixon, had spent a semester and a half at Yale before seizing the opportunity for some world

travel. The senator, a passenger, engaged him in an
extended debate over several days as the train sped on its
way to California. In the process they discussed
thoroughly the "most debated points of the race question
[such] as the relative mentality, physical and facial
beauty, sex instinct, chastity, odor, truthfulness, health,
honesty, of Negro and Caucasian; as well as politics, the
slavery of white people in Colonial America and elswhere,
intermarriage, religion, ancient Negro civilization, race
attraction and repulsion, lynching and other aspects all
scientifically dealt with...."[30]

From Superman to Man was reviewed and re-reviewed
several times in the *Negro World*. Hubert H. Harrison
called it in 1920 "the greatest little book on the Negro"
that he had read.[31] His *Negro World* remarks still adorn
the book's dust jacket over a half century later. In 1922
Harrison again discussed the book, this time in the context
of Black intellectuals' dereliction of their duty towards
aspiring Black writers. "During the period from 1917 to
the present," he wrote, "this book has made its way to
success without one word of encouragement or praise from
any of the more prominent Negro writers or editors except
Mr. Ferris and myself...." Free copies, he said, had been
sent to W.E.B. DuBois, Kelly Miller, Benjamin Brawley,
William Monroe Trotter, W.S. Scarborough, W.S. Braithwaite and others, but to little or no avail. Rogers had also
sent copies to the NAACP in Chicago and New York
"under the curious delusion that an Association for the
Advancement of Colored People would like to hear of a
book in which the cause of colored people was so well
advanced." Brawley was one of the few who had even
bothered to acknowledge receipt but he "as usual, was too
stupid to form any critical opinion worth a tinker's
dam...." Arthur A. Schomburg and John Edward Bruce
were the only persons of this class to offer encouragement,
apart from Harrison and Ferris.

Harrison contrasted the attitudes of the Black middle class literati with those of poor Black people, liberal whites, and even racist whites like "Vardaman, of Mississippi, whom the book attacked" and who nevertheless "sent a courteous note of acknowledgement." Ordinary Black folk were the real heroes of the book's success. Many had volunteered to sell copies, often refusing remuneration in the process. As of 1922 they were still making the "pilgrimage" to Rogers' place at 513 Lenox Avenue to obtain copies.

The silly and damaging antics of the Black middle class were a favorite theme of Harrison's, one to which he returned time and again in the pages of the *Negro World*. Rogers' experience now provided him with a useful point of departure for this discussion. Harrison was a good friend of Claude McKay, and he could not help but compare their similar experiences. Harrison's observations here were later corroborated by McKay himself in his autobiography, *A Long Way From Home*. "When Claude McKay erupted into notice," Harrison observed bitterly, "these colored pseudo-intellectuals couldn't tell from reading his poems that he was worth noticing. But now that their superiors have spoken they take Claude out to lunch and lionize him 'most much.' As with McKay, so with Rogers. As soon as these copy-cats shall have learned from their teachers how great is 'From Superman to Man,' they will slobber over him and give space to his book." "Who," Harrison concluded, paraphrasing a Latin quotation, "shall put brains in our brainy men?"[32]

Hodge Kirnon, another *Negro World* regular, called Rogers' work "the intellectual supplement to the spiritual side of Garveyism."[33] Harrison would have agreed, for he had earlier discussed Garvey's early struggles to establish the *Negro World* in terms similar to his commentary on Rogers' early efforts. When Garvey began work on the paper "the so-called educated people of the race

spurned it.... Several of the poor people of the race came
to his rescue and donated about one thousand dollars to
finance the *Negro World*. Garvey could not pay an editor;
he edited, managed and distributed the paper himself."[34]

Rogers' second book, *As Nature Leads* (1920) and other
works were also reviewed in the *Negro World*. In 1922 he
published "The Unconquerable Maroons" serially in the
paper, which called it "Positively the most sensational tale
of the race to protect itself from the lust and licentiousness
and savage cruelty of white civilization!"[35] Rogers
sometimes lectured to UNIA audiences and *From
Superman to Man* was offered free with *Negro World*
subscriptions as late as 1927.[36]

Carter G. Woodson had much in common with Rogers.
He, too, was a prolific historian. And despite a Harvard
Ph.D. he, too, found white publishing houses closed to
him. Like Rogers, he resorted to publishing his own work,
in his case via his Associated Publishers. Rogers and
Harrison became good friends. Woodson was acquainted
with *Negro World* regulars Bruce and Schomburg.

Woodson is best remembered as founder of the
Association for the Study of Afro-American (formerly
"Negro") Life and History in 1915; and also for the
association's *Journal of Negro History* which first ap-
peared in 1916. In 1926 he introduced the celebration of
Negro History Week (now Black History Month).

Woodson's books were reviewed in the *Negro World*
and he and his work were subject to frequent comments. A
spate of such commentary took place in 1922 when he
accepted a grant of $50,000 from the Carnegie and
Rockefeller foundations. Robert L. Poston acknowledged
the predicament that Woodson found himself in.
Woodson's cause was worthy and his funds were
inadequate. Who was he to counsel Woodson against
taking the money in such circumstances? He implored
Woodson, though, to be careful, "For nothing could have

a more harmful effect on the Negro than a Negro history dictated by white capitalists." Ferris expressed the same concern, and a *Negro World* editorial commended Woodson on the gift while harboring the same reservations.[37]

The concern expressed over this gift was rooted in the doctrine of Black self-reliance, one of the ideological rocks upon which the UNIA was built. It was consistent with this position when, in 1927, *Negro World* columnist S. A. Haynes rushed to the support of Woodson in his effort to independently raise $20,000 "for the perpetuation of Negro History." "We are now informed by Dr. Carter Woodson, brilliant historian," Haynes wrote, that only $6,294.27 had been raised. He continued,

> This is an astounding revelation. Millions of useless churches, millions for white-controlled theatres, dance halls, cabarets, and industries, millions to the Jews for fine clothes, millions to the white insurance companies and banks in whose corporate body no Negro presides; millions for the frivolities of life, but not twenty thousand dollars to perpetuate the glory and splendor of our past and present achievements. Where is our pride, our love of self, our conception of vision and intelligence?
>
> ... The Negro rightly demands life, liberty and the pursuit of happiness - but a race that doesn't know where it came from doesn't know where it is going; and it is dangerous for such a race to possess these virtues minus this important compass.[38]

Yet, in formal reviews, Woodson's books did not receive the unqualified praise that had been accorded to Rogers. Ferris thought his *History of the Negro Church* "On the whole... a splendid general survey of the development of the Negro church," but one in which there were, nevertheless, "grave sins of omission...."[39]

Schomburg was even harsher on Woodson in his review of *The Negro in Our History*. This was one of the longest formal reviews ever published in the *Negro World* and went into exhaustive detail. Schomburg was a specialist collector of rare Africana and his knowledge of obscure sources was legendary. These he cited extensively to show that Woodson's book was "not based on a careful examination and research of the sources, but rather on speculative opinion and findings of latter-day writers." He challenged Woodson's assertions that Africa had originally been peopled by mulattoes; that Denmark Vesey, the slave revolutionary, was born in San Domingo (as opposed to St. Thomas); and that slavery was milder in the West Indies than in the United States. In conclusion he found *The Negro In Our History* to be "splendidly and profusely illustrated, but unfortunately out of tune with the rules of chronology. There is much information promiscuously scattered through the 342 pages for those who may want to read and enjoy the 'dry bones of history.'"[40]

Both Schomburg and Bruce had apparently provided Woodson with illustrations for the book, in the name of the Negro Society for Historical Research, which they had founded in 1911. They regretted the absence of any acknowledgement. Said Schomburg, acidly, "A charitable appreciation for those who helped Dr. Woodson with rare prints, engravings, etc., would not have in any way harmed him in the preface. It is one of the few books lacking this feature of long-established custom."[41] Bruce reviewed the book for Garvey's *Daily Negro Times*.[42]

Woodson did not let these reviews prevent him from approaching Garvey to publish in the *Negro World*. T.Thomas Fortune answered for Garvey - "Your letter...addressed to Mr. Garvey, was referred to me. I have deemed it good to publish the synopsis of Miss Sanborn's book, as sent us by you, in the magazine section of the Negro World of January 5."[43]

Several years later, in 1931 and 1932, Woodson published a regular weekly column in the *Negro World*. Many of these articles were republished in book form in his celebrated polemic, *The Mis-Education of the Negro* (1933). In a vein reminiscent of Harrison's articles, Woodson inveighed heavily against "genuflecting Negroes," "Negroes of the obsequious type," "racial toadies" and white "traducers of the Negro race." Amy Jacques Garvey quoted extensively from a Woodson *Negro World* article in her biography of her husband.[44]

Woodson's was not the only book that had its genesis, at least in part, in the *Negro World*. Another was *Some Essentials of Race Leadership* (1924) by Arnold Hamilton Maloney, a former assistant chaplain general of the UNIA and psychology professor at Wilberforce University. Some of these essays, too, had appeared originally in the *Negro World*. The book received two favorable reviews.

The *Negro World* reviewers were as talented and insightful as any to be found anywhere. Their willingness to publish multiple reviews of the same work and their ability to supplement formal reviews with less formal commentary enabled them to do an unusually thorough job. All manner of authors, famous and unknown, white and Black, could get a hearing. These included Garvey himself, whose *Philosophy and Opinions of Marcus Garvey*, edited by Amy Jacques Garvey, received a respectful review from Ferris in 1923. "At present Marcus Garvey is discussed pro and con," Ferris began. "He is not yet forty years old and yet judgement is being pronounced upon his life work."[45]

6

Music, Drama, Art
and Elocution

Literature is largely indivisible from music and the other arts. At a group level, interest in one normally influences interest in the others. At the individual level, also, interest in one aspect of the arts often spills over into others. Augusta Savage, as already noted, was sculptor, portrait painter and poet. Among the better-known Harlem Renaissance personalities, Langston Hughes combined poetry, fiction, non-fiction and an interest in jazz; James Weldon Johnson wrote poetry and wrote on music and the theatre.

Garvey's own "renaissance" was no different. Pageantry played an important role within the UNIA. And music was an integral part of UNIA meetings. As of 1920, the headquarters Liberty Hall in Harlem supported a UNIA Band and Orchestra and a Band of the African Legion, both under the direction of Professor Arnold J. Ford. Ford also directed the Liberty Hall Choir (also known as the Universal Choir). Completing the picture was the Black Star Line Band led by Professor William Isles.[1] Non-UNIA talent was also sought at Liberty Hall. Women's day at the 1922 convention featured "America's Greatest Contralto Soloist," Marian Anderson.[2]

Other UNIA divisions also had their own choirs and orchestras. The Indianapolis UNIA choir in 1922 was said to be the best choir in the city and one of the best UNIA choirs anywhere.[3] When Garvey moved back to Jamaica in 1927, he took with him his interest in music and theatre. The result was the Universal Jazz Hounds, a choir and the UNIA Follies.[4] Several of Jamaica's well-known entertainers of later years are said to have gotten their start at Garvey's Edelweis Park performances.

The UNIA had an anthem, the "Universal Ethiopian Anthem," part compsed by Ford. Ford also wrote the words and music for "God Bless Our President," a hymn in praise of Garvey and composed the "Legion's Marching Song," anthem of the paramilitary Universal African Legions -

> The Legion here, will fight for Africa there,
> We are going to avenge her wrongs,
> We are coming, oh, Mother Africa,
> We are four hundred millions strong....
>
> We shall fight our foe, from coast to coast,
> For Africa must be free,
> I am a soldier, Mother Africa,
> You can depend on me.
>
> Travel on, on, on, my good brother,
> And keep within the law,
> No cracker will dare to slap our Mother,
> Or we will knock him on the jaw.
>
> No cracker will dare to seduce our sister,
> Or to hang us on a limb,
> And we are not obliged to call him mister,
> Or to skin our lips at him.

Some *Negro World* poets also set their verses to music. One of them, a Mrs. Maud Semper, had set her Garvey acrostic to music by August, 1920. "Already," the paper reported, "three songs have been composed and set to music in honor of the UNIA." It added, not untruthfully, that "When a movement can inspire songs and poetry it shows that it has touched the hearts of men."[5] Bandmaster Isles also published a musical tribute to Garvey entitled "Our Leader - March Song."[6]

Garvey himself wrote songs of various description. He

wrote "Keep Cool" while incarcerated in Atlanta in 1927. Alexander Seymour wrote the music.[7] An advertisement described it as the "Song Hit of the Season" and it was said to have been proclaimed a success by *The Music Trade News*. In 1934, Garvey published his *Universal Negro Improvement Association Convention Hymns*. This included hymns written by both Garvey and Arnold J. Ford together with some traditional numbers. Garvey could not resist mixing race uplift with religion and so his hymns seemed to have more to do with slavery and African liberation than with God.[8]

During the UNIA's Seventh International Convention in Jamaica in 1934, several of Garvey's poems were "most admirably set to music by Mr. B. de C. Reid" and rendered by a choir.[9]

The UNIA recorded some of its music on phonograph records. Two were available in 1921. One featured, E.W. Bradley singing the "Universal Ethiopian Anthem" accompanied by the Black Star Line Band. A sacred quartette did "Shine On Eternal Light" on the flip side. The other featured an instrumental version of the "Universal Ethiopian Anthem" by the Black Star Line Band, with the band doing "Hostrauser's March" on the other side. A third record featured two speeches by Garvey.[10]

UNIA music was good music - good enough to impress a critical outsider from a rival organization with its "exceptionally fine quality."[11] Liberty Hall soloists, such as Mme M.B. Houston, were reputed very good. And in Arnold J. Ford and William Isles, Garvey was able to find two highly talented musical directors.

Ford, a Barbadian, had served in the musical corps of the British Royal Navy during World War I. He played several instruments and was a prolific composer (both words and music) of songs sacred and secular. He edited the *Universal Ethiopian Hymnal* (1920) which included some of his own compositions. In 1930, he emigrated to Ethiopia with a group of Garveyites and Black Jews (among whom he was a rabbi).[12]

Ford's lyrics (as witness the "Legion's Marching Song") revealed quite clearly his willingness to harness music to the service of struggle. His work was a comprehensive reflection of the Garvey aesthetic. His lyrics further gave evidence of wide learning, especially in African history. His best known song, the "Universal Ethiopian Anthem," was composed in 1919 and adopted as the offical anthem of the race at Garvey's First International Convention of the Negro Peoples of the World in 1920. It began,

> Ethiopia, thou land of our fathers,
> Thou land where the gods loved to be,
> As storm cloud at night suddenly gathers
> Our armies come rushing to thee.
> We must in the fight be victorious
> When swords are thrust outward to gleam;
> For us will the victory be glorious
> When led by the red, black and green.
>
> Chorus
>
> Advance, advance to victory,
> Let Africa be free;
> Advance to meet the foe
> With the might
> Of the red, the black and the green....[13]

The increasingly popular jazz music found an appreciative audience in Liberty Hall, as witness the name of the Jamaican Universal Jazz Hounds. But both Ford and Isles came to the UNIA with training and experience in a variety of musical modes, including classical music. Isles especially was concerned that Black musicians and composers should strive for a level of perfection in no way inferior to the best of what other people had to offer, "from Beethoven downward," as he put it.

Isles brought to bear on his Liberty Hall job not only

thorough knowledge of the technical aspects of music, but
a vast knowledge of the history of music as it developed on
many continents. To all this he added a personal commitment to Marcus Garvey and a deep attachment to the
goals of his organization. The *Negro World* said of him -
"Mr. Isles is an indefatigable student and is able to
combine art and propaganda...in a remarkably congenial
way."[14]

In 1922, the *Negro World* carried Isles' six-part series of
articles on "The Negro and Music," which he hoped
eventually to work into a book. Isles explored the sources
of Black music as far back as ancient Egypt and surveyed
the musical histories of India, China, Mesopotamia and
other places. He also displayed a wide knowledge of Black
musicians in European history. He even explored the
psychology of music.

As a New Negro and a Garveyite, Isles had some interesting things to say about slave songs or "jubilee"
music. He recognized that slave songs were an important
part of the Black musical heritage. They represented a
historical reality that must not be forgotten. But he
resented efforts to fossilize Black music at this particular
point in its development. Much as the *Negro World* poets
stayed away from dialect poetry, so too did Isles frown
upon the attempted revival of slave songs - and for similar
reasons. He distrusted the motives of those who felt
comforted by the vision of darkies singing plaintive
melodies in the cotton fields.

"Not that I detest these songs," Isles emphasized.
"God forbid! They were born out of the suffering souls of
our foreparents. That we should forget them? No! I can
hear those chants as they rose from their bruised and
beaten bodies. That the melody of the work songs should
be discarded? No! I can again hear the syncopated
rhythms as they flow from the banjo." Yet, he objected to
anyone "encouraging the singing of these songs daily in

our institutions," and also to "having them thrust
wholesale upon us in the form of jubiliee singers, etc."
"Let me begin to sing the following Negro slave song," he
concluded, "which was given much publicity and encouragement in some of our papers:

> I kin fill dis baskit if I choose,
> Den Massa gwine give me Christmas shoes,
> Two red han'k'chief an' a walking cane,
> Den I'se gwine strut down de Big house lane.

and immediately there will be a battle between the spirit
of freedom within and the spirit of slavery trying to enter.
The soul of this new Manhood Race of ours rebels against
such utterances."[15]

The African-English composer, Samuel Coleridge-
Taylor, seemed to Isles to embody the qualities of
technical proficiency and race perspective which he ad-
mired. He considered Coleridge-Taylor "the most
cultured musician of his race...a man of the highest
aesthetic ideals, who sought to give permanence to the
folksongs of his people by giving them a new interpretation and added dignity."[16] Isles was referring
here specifically to Coleridge-Taylor's *Twenty-Four Negro
Melodies* in which the composer provided variations of
folk-songs from Africa, Afro-America and the Caribbean.
"What Brahms has done for the Hungarian folk-music,
Dvorak for the Bohemian and Grieg for the Norweigian,"
Coleridge-Taylor had written, "I have tried to do for these
Negro melodies."[17] Coleridge-Taylor represented for
Isles, the continuing quest for "new areas to develop, new
musical heights to scale." This was much preferable to
stagnation at one point in ones historical development.

Isles brought his six-part series to a grand finale which
was remarkable alike for its eloquence as for its attempt to
relate the Garvey aesthetic to music. He wrote,

In the onward march of progress the Negro has evolved upon a new and higher plane of human affairs, whether they be science, art, literature or music. His eyes are open to behold the dawn of a new era pregnant with possibilities and full of hope. He is determined that nothing shall deter him from his objective. He shall not be dragged backwards, and the vicissitudes of life through which he has passed shall not only be history but be regarded as milestones in the march towards his goal. The old adage of "Servants, obey your masters," will make of you nothing more than a servant. Therefore, in conclusion I say, let us march on. On to the highest heights of human development. We have had the experience of a hundred battlefields. Let us convert them into grand martial strains which shall ring from a thousand bands and fire us to do or die. We have seen life and all its tragedies. Let us convert them into operas and draw out of our men and women that genius which is so latent within them. Our souls are receptive to nature and all its beauties. The singing of birds, the trickling of the brook, the blooming of flowers and the grandeur of the landscape - let it give outburst in music, a new music born of a free being, free in mind, free in body and free in soul.[18]

Isles' ideas on the type of music befitting New Negroes were shared by other Garveyites. R. L. Poston used an editorial to express his disgust at the embarrassing stuff that was being passed off as genuine jubilee music.[19] Ferris agreed in essence with Isles and Poston, though differing slightly in emphasis. He seemed marginally more willing than the others to put plantation songs behind him. He was eager for the race to demonstrate its ability to master even the most technically demanding western music. "Dvorak, the Bohemian composer, said that the songs of Negro slaves was America's only real contribution to music," he wrote, " and we are proud of that fact. But we also aspire for greater things. " He was glad to note that "the Negro is now developing real musicians, musicians who can master melody and harmony as well as rhythm, syncopation and jazz." He was full of praise for Isle's Black Star Line Band, which had provided interesting interpretations of classical pieces - "And on armistice night, in Liberty Hall, New York City, over two thousand persons applauded the singers and the Black Star Line Band until the rafters of the roof echoed back the sound. One of the numbers that made a hit and called for an encore was Verdi's 'Il Trovatore,' sung by two colored singers in a manner worthy of grand opera stars."[20]

UNIA literary and artistic activity naturally extended into the field of drama. Garvey himself is known to have written and produced plays. His *The Coronation of the African King*, in three acts, was performed at his Edelweis Park headquarters in Jamaica in 1930. The play presented the rise of anti-colonial consciousness in Africa since 1918 as a result of UNIA propaganda.[21] As an interesting aside, Garvey's estranged first wife, Amy Ashwood Garvey, authored and produced three musical comedies in New York in 1926 and 1927. At least two of them played at Harlem's Lafayette Theatre. They were *Hey, Hey!*, *Brown Sugar* and *Black Magic*.[22]

UNIA locals often wrote and staged their own plays. Always, these productions were designed to explain and further the goals of the organization. UNIA ladies in Harlem in 1924 sponsored *From Peasant to Crown Prince of Egypt*, a drama set in the reign of the Pharoah Tut-Ankh-Amen.[23] ("King Tut's" tomb had only recently been discovered and had generated much discussion in the *Negro World* concerning the African origins of civilization).

The Black Cross Nurses (a UNIA auxiliary) of Norfolk, Virginia staged *An African Convention*, a play that "was full of race pride, and was staged to enthuse the public on the aims of the UNIA and ACL." In Newport News, Virginia, at about the same time, the juvenile Black Cross Nurses and Boy Scouts (of the UNIA) staged a "playlet" entitled *Coming Home to Africa.*[24]

In 1921, *The New Negro*, "A Genuine Negro Melodrama," played in Philadelphia under the auspices of the local UNIA. The author, A. Lincoln Harris, incorporated several UNIA officials, including Garvey, into his list of characters. In the play Garvey's son falls in love with an Indian girl, Waena. Waena and her brother were separated from their mother at an early age and a white man who knew them from infancy is the only one who knows their parentage. The children themselves have no recollection of their mother. Garvey objects to his son's marriage outside of the race since he wants the boy to continue his life's work after his death. Mrs. Garvey, however, is willing to let love triumph, and she gets her son a marriage license. But Garvey is adamant. He arrives on the scene just in time to stop the marriage. The white man at this point remembers that he knew Waena and her brother as infants. He recalls that they are not Indians at all, but Black. They all presumably live happily ever after.

Even a "melodrama" such as this was not without its message. "The old Uncle Tom type," commented the *Negro World*, "is shown as a servant of the Hon. Marcus Garvey, while the New Negro stands up man to man in the son of Marcus Garvey and demands an equal break with other races."[25]

John Edward Bruce also tried his hand at play writing. His *Preaching vs. Practice* had as its main characters a bank manager, a "very suave" Baptist preacher and some New Negroes, who happened to be UNIA members.[26] Another Bruce creation, *Which One*, revolved around an African UNIA diplomat, Sennebundo Ajai. Three young ladies were in love with Ajai, one each from Martinique, the Anglophone Caribbean and Afro-America. Ajai found himself in the pleasant predicament of having to choose one of these ladies. Some of the action took place in the

UNIA offices that Bruce knew so well, and against a back-drop of the Garveyite colors of red, black and green. Ajai was eventually able to make up his mind before leaving on an organizing trip to Nigeria. He and his bride-to-be planned to be married in a Liberty Hall in Africa.[27] (Garvey's first marriage had taken place in Liberty Hall in Harlem). Bruce also authored short stories, including one, "The Odious Comparison," which was serialized in the *Negro World* in 1922.

Bruce's authorship of these plays emphasizes a point which has been demonstrated already in the case of poetry, literary criticism and literature and the arts in general. UNIA officials, from Garvey on down, participated actively in the organization's cultural activity. They lived in the era of the Harlem Renaissance and they themselves were "renaissance" men and women in an older sense - people of broad learning and culture for whom literature and the arts were as much a part of their everyday existence as were race uplift and politics. Their educational backgrounds varied. Ferris was a graduate of Harvard and Yale. R.L. Poston graduated from Howard University. Harrison was a self-taught man who was accepted as an equal in the community of scholars. Garvey was largely self-taught. He had attended some law lectures at Birkbeck College in London, but was not a college graduate. Bruce was born a slave but was able to attend public schools after the United States Civil War. Yet, by whatever varied means, they all attained to a level of artistic, scholarly and political interest which was quite remarkable.

All of this is borne out in the case of "the great race drama" *Tallaboo*, staged by the UNIA Dramatic Club in January of 1922. The play was the work of the late N.R. Harper of Kentucky and was directed by the Poston brothers, Robert and Ulysses, and Lester Taylor, a regular contributor to the paper. The cast of thirty-nine included several UNIA and *Negro World* officials and their spouses, including Ulysses Poston and Mrs. J.E. Bruce.

Tallaboo was designed in part to "Interpret the Ideas of This Great Association" and, according to Ferris' review, it succeeded admirably. It was a well-constructed play with a message, but not a forced message; in other words, it was Ferris' kind of propaganda play. "In 'Tallaboo,' " he noted, "the lesson of race pride and race respect is taught in a natural and spontaneous manner. 'Tallaboo' is not heavy and labored as so many race novels and plays are. But the story runs easily and naturally. The characters are strong and interesting. The audience enjoys the play as a play. And after it is all over the spectator realizes that his racial vision has been broadened and his racial ideals uplifted." *Tallaboo* won equal praise from Dusé Mohamed Ali (himself a playwright and former actor), A. Lincoln Harris, author of *The New Negro*, N.R. Harper's son, who made a special trip to New York for the occasion, and Marcus Garvey himself. [28]

The *Negro World* also carried regular notices of non-UNIA plays and the commercial theatre scene in Harlem and elsewhere. A 1922 editorial welcomed the opening up of Broadway to such Black shows as *Shuffle Along, Strut Miss Lizzie* and *The Plantation Revue*. Yet it felt that places like the Lafayette Theatre in Harlem were where the best Black productions were still to be seen. [29]

Besides, this new white interest in Black productions was bound to excite some suspicion in Garveyite circles. The New Negro who frowned on white "dialect" poetry and spurious jubilee songs was not likely to appreciate "a Negro comedian with blackened face, red lips and grotesque garb, shuffling and shambling and galloping and cavorting on the stage or playing 'Emperor Jones.' "

The above observation came from Ferris, in response to

an article by Jessie Fauset in the *Crisis*. Fauset had
noticed, disapprovingly, that "among many theatre goers
Charles Gilpin's rendition of the Emperor Jones caused a
deep sense of irritation. They could not distinguish between the artistic interpretation of a type and the
deliberate travestying of a race, and so their appreciation
was clouded."

Ferris disagreed. Like the lady who had remonstrated
with Harrison on this same subject, he did not think that
access to Broadway and white recognition was worth the
price, if the price was to be continuous defamation on the
stage. The average Black person, he argued, did not
necessarily object per se to the "Uncle Toms, the
mammies the pickaninnies, the buck and wing dancers,
etc." But why should this type of character not be
balanced by plays on "Toussaint L'Ouverture, Sir William
Conrad Reeves, Henry Highland Garnet, William Howard
Day, Frederick Douglass, Alexander Crummell, Edward
Wilmot Blyden, Dusé Mohamed [Ali], Marcus Garvey,
William Monroe Trotter and Dr. W.E.B. DuBois?" Surely
these men were "as worthy of presentation on the stage as
the banjo players and 'Shuffle Along' dancers."[30]

It was this kind of thinking that had led Garvey to his
1930s campaign against Paul Robeson who, it will be
remembered, replaced Charles Gilpin in the title role for
the movie version of *The Emperor Jones*. Some of
Robeson's other stage and movie roles, such as *Sanders of
the River* and *Stevedore* were equally unflattering to the
race. Robeson was by this time the most celebrated Black
actor of the period and Garvey did not take kindly to one in
his position being used in such a demeaning way. Garvey
and Robeson were both living in London by this time, so
Garvey had ample opportunity to monitor the actor's
career. "Paul Robeson, the Negro actor, has left London
for Hollywood," Garvey announced in 1935. "He is gone

there to make another slanderous picture against the
Negro." Garvey argued, like Ferris, that success in white
circles should not automatically and uncritically ensure
Black acceptance. He hoped that Robeson would at least
benefit financially from his acting, "so that when he
retires from the stage he may be able to square his conscience with his race by doing something good for it."[31]

In 1937 Garvey complained to the British Moving
Picture Board about Robeson's films and in 1939 he
published a pamphlet with the imposing title of *Grand
Speech of Hon. Marcus Garvey at Kingsway Hall, London,
Denouncing the Moving Picture Propaganda to Discredit
the Negro.* This pamphlet he described as "A Criticism of
Paul Robeson in Pictures."[32]

Garvey was far from alone in his reaction to the film
version of *Emperor Jones.* A *Negro World* writer covering
the film's Harlem premiere in 1933 reported that the
audience did not like it at all. They resented "the fact that
such a brilliant man as Paul Robeson should have to stoop
to giving an interpretation of such a sordid soul."[33]

Several years before all this, Robeson's penchant for
landing such roles had almost brought him into an even
more direct collision with Garvey and the UNIA. For it was
reported in 1929 that plans were afoot for the staging of
Jeremiah the Magnificent,   said to have been written by
Wallace Thurman and Willard Jourdan Rapp and based on
the career of Marcus Garvey. The producers were said to
be seeking Robeson for the title role in this play of the
"sensational dramatic type."[34] Thurman, whom the
Negro World reporter mistakenly identified as white, and
Rapp (who was in fact white) had collaborated on the 1929
production, *Harlem.*

There was a happy ending of sorts to the Robeson story.
Robeson did eventually tire of demeaning roles (and,
perhaps, of Black criticism). He decided to sever his

connection with Hollywood in 1939. He had discovered late, but better late than never, that "they will never let me play a part in a film in which a Negro is on top."[35] Now he was ready "to square his conscience with his race by doing something good for it."

Non-commercial, non-UNIA drama also came under the purview of UNIA criticism. In December 1921 Dusé Mohamed Ali witnessed a play staged by the Dunbar Players in Washington, D.C. It upset him so much that he wrote a whole review of it without mentioning what the name of the play was. The players produced "third-rate white melodrama," he complained, "instead of plays by black playwrights on black subjects." Their white-face was ludicrous. And if they insisted on white plays, then why not at least do something educationally worthwhile, like Shakespeare?

Ali disliked the players as much as he disliked their unnamed play. "I think they are misusing the name of Dunbar," he said. "If Dunbar stood for anything he stood for all that was best in the Negro, and it must not be forgotten that Dunbar was black, whereas the Dunbar Players are colored men and women who try to look as white as they possibly can on the stage." Ali could not separate the Dunbar Players from the type of drama they performed any more than he would have separated the UNIA Dramatic Club from *Tallaboo*. He found the Dunbar Players "as amusing in their way as the people who straighten their hair and bleach their complexions, because, although colored, their outlook is white, and until the Negro shall realize that he has been somebody and will be somebody again, maintaining a separate entity, he is likely to remain in his present condition of semi-serfdom, dependence and spinelessness."[36]

Ali here sounded almost more Garveyite than Garvey.

But the basis of artistic criticism for the New Negro was, ultimately, political. And here he merely expressed, very forthrightly, even angrily, the political basis of UNIA criticism.

In the field of art, the UNIA could claim as its own the sculptor Augusta Savage, as previously noted. Garvey himself collected African artwork.[37] James Van Der Zee, one of Afro-America's greatest photographers, did a lot of work around the movement. His UNIA photographs appeared in the *Negro World* and have been reprinted many times since.[38]

The *Negro World*, through its association with the UNIA, was able to supplement its interest in writing with access to some of the best of the spoken word. The UNIA boasted an unusually able corps of public speakers. Garvey himself had made a study of elocution from his youth in Jamaica. He had won elocution contests there from as early as 1910. In its first Jamaican days (1914-1916), the UNIA sponsored elocution contests, at least one of which Garvey entered and won. He met his first wife in 1914 at a debate. (She was principal speaker and he supported her from the floor). In the 1930s he again organized elocution contests in Jamaica. Many were the words of praise heaped upon Garvey, throughout his public life, for the excellence of his oratory. Friends and foes alike testified to this fact.[39]

Henrietta Vinton Davis, fourth assistant president-general of the UNIA, had been a nationally and internationally known elocutionist long before she joined Garvey. As a clerk in the office of the recorder of deeds (the first Black woman ever appointed there), she was encouraged to study elocution by Frederick Douglass. Douglass was on hand to introduce her at her debut performance in Washington.[40] Claude McKay called her "one of the finest elocutionists of the Negro group and a very sensitive interpreter of Shakespearean roles at home and abroad."[41]

Along with its reviews of written work, the *Negro World* also carried the occasional review of a dramatic recital. Dusé Mohamed Ali attended such a performance by Madame Maud Jones and pronounced it the best he had heard in his thirty-nine years of "dramatic and literary experience." He liked her as much as he disliked the Dunbar Players. "Her tones are musical," he enthused, "her expression intensely dramatic...her technique and artistry surmount many of the most difficult cadences in the elocutionary register." Were she "Caucasianized" she surely would have been accorded the universal acclaim she deserved.[42]

Formal debates, also, followed the UNIA from Jamaica to the United States. Some of these debates were written rather than oral and took the form of extended dialogues between *Negro World* editors. Such a debate took place in 1920 between Harrison and Bruce, arising out of Harrison's disagreement with some sentiment expressed in his colleague's column. The paper's readers joined in, via their letters to the editor.[43]

A similar debate took place in 1922 between T. Thomas Fortune, then editing Garvey's *Daily Negro Times*, and Ferris. This exchange took place mostly in the *Negro World* but spilled over into its sister paper as well. The topic of debate was the highly unlikely one of "miracles." It started innocently enough. Ferris, in a speech at Liberty Hall (with Garvey present) stated that the days of physical miracles were over. His remarks were reprinted in the *Negro World* and seem to have caught Fortune in a contentious mood.

Fortune soon replied, via the *Daily Negro Times*, that

miracles were happening all around Ferris. Liberty Hall
was itself a miracle. For had it not come into being
through the "miraculous influence of Mr. Marcus Garvey?" "The Universal Negro Improvement Association
could not have been created," he added, "except by a
physical miracle produced by a physical body containing a
miraculous spirit." And electric light and aeroplanes were
miracles too.

As in all good arguments, the differences seemed to be
more semantic than real. Ferris preferred to define a
miracle as "a transgression of a law of nature by a particular volition of the Deity." When the sun stood still or
Jesus turned water into wine, there you had real miracles.
All he had really meant to say in the first place was that
African peoples would have to harness nature and
discipline themselves, like other races had done - "we
need not expect that the Almighty will dispatch Michael,
Gabriel or other angels with flaming swords and
chariots...to redeem Africa."[44] So even so esoteric a topic
as miracles turned out to be a discussion on the redemption of Africa. Even here the Garvey aesthetic seemed at
work.

These debates always remained good-natured. But, like
the phenomenon of multiple reviews of a single work, or
like the varied explorations of the place of propaganda in
art, they revealed a high commitment to democratic
practice within the organization. This was a democratic
practice, however, that revolved around the principles laid
down by Marcus Garvey.

H.G. Mudgal, himself later a *Negro World* editor,
satirized the Fortune-Ferris debate in a pretty bad poem
entitled "The Miracle (With Apology to the Editor of The
Negro Times and The Literary Editor of the Negro
World)"-

> When two editors fight
> With all their might
> And make a spectacle -
> Yea! 'tis a miracle....[45]

Mudgal it was who, in the 1930s, popularized the practice of debates against rival organizations, with himself as principal defender of the UNIA. The audience was judge and whoever was up against the UNIA usually lost, though debates sometimes took place on neutral territory. Various communists lost such debates, as did the Black conservative George S. Schuyler.[46] Garvey won a similar formal debate against a communist opponent at his 1929 International Convention in Jamaica.[47]

The Defectors - Eric Walrond
and Claude McKay

Garvey's wider political movement inevitably attracted its fair share of opportunists. Here was a massive movement - the most massive of its kind in history - whose leaders were in the limelight and whose coffers were overflowing. At a time when many Black university graduates were lucky if they could find employment as Pullman porters, here was a Black organization with the wherewithal to employ many of its own in positions commensurate with their training.

And Garvey was ever on the lookout for Black talent. Many were the convention delegates who journeyed to Harlem from Panama, from Sierra Leone, from Detroit, from Grenada, from anywhere, and who were offered jobs by Garvey on the spot.[1] They had only to demonstrate their ability, to excite his interest. The converse was also true. Black folk with unusual skills knew in advance that they would find an enthusiastic welcome from the UNIA and they often headed straight for Garvey's office upon their arrival in New York. It is no coincidence that the first Black aviator in the United States and the first to captain a ship in the United States merchant marine both passed through the UNIA.[2]

Many of these people were of course honest and tried to put as much into the organization as they got from it. Those who were opportunists, however, fell into three categories. First there were those who were in it primarily for the exposure and the money. They were able to utilize these benefits for later careers in politics, law, business, real estate, writing and the like. A second group was basically sincere but simply did not have the stamina to stick it out when governmental and other repression descended upon the organization. A third group consisted of some who Garvey recruited on account of their scarce skills. They were willing to work for Garvey, but they never caught the vision of his movement. Theirs was simply a job, like any other. and if the opportunity arose, they could easily be swayed to do what was wrong.

It has happened more than once in the course of Black history that the masses have created openings for the race that they themselves have lacked the skills to fill. It happened often in the 1960s, when professorships in white universities and positions in government and private industry opened up for Black people as a result of mass pressure. The problem then, as for the Garvey Movement, was, "How do you make the beneficiaries of mass struggle accountable to the masses?"

No workable answers were forthcoming to this question in the Afro-America of the 1960s and 1970s. No adequate answer was forthcoming in the time of Garvey. A case in point is provided by Captain Joshua Cockburn of the Black Star Line. He was one of the few Black persons in the world with a master's license, and Garvey desperately needed such a person to captain the line's first ship. Cockburn joined the Black Star Line but soon succumbed to graft and corruption and did his share towards wrecking the company. Then he testified against Garvey at the celebrated mail fraud trial of 1923.[3]

The same pattern could be seen in the UNIA's literary operations, and Eric Walrond was the worst offender. Zora Neale Hurston's post-*Negro World* references to Garvey were as scurrilous, perhaps more so. But Hurston, though published in the Garvey organ, seems never to have claimed to be a Garveyite. In Walrond's case it was different.

Walrond's editorials began appearing in the *Negro World* shortly before publication of the results of the 1921 literary competition. It may be that Garvey had already read his entry and offered him a job in anticipation of making the results public. A Walrond editorial appeared in the very issue of the paper in which the results of the competition were announced.[4] Though there were several categories for essays in the competition, the one that Walrond chose, "Africa Redeemed," seems to have been considered the stellar category. At least it received the biggest headlines, and this was one of the categories that Garvey personally judged.

The announcement of the competition results coincided with Walrond's formal inclusion among the editorial page credits. Thereafter, his articles increased rapidly. He became a prolific contributor of book and other reviews, short stories and features, in addition to editorials, both signed and unsigned. For a while, he seemed to be Garvey's chief defender among the editorial writers. Even before the competition results were published, he had editorially criticized W.E.B. DuBois' Pan-African Congress in the name of "clear-thinking exponents of Garveyism."[5] In a later editorial he gave a spirited exposition of the race first and self-reliance principles that underpinned the Garvey aesthetic. "After the European War," he wrote, "the Negroes of the world realized that they could not put up with the clap-trap being ladled out to them by the leaders of the NAACP, Tuskegee Institute and the myriad other associations 'founded in the interest of colored people,' but directed and financed by philanthropists who did not know the Negro intimately. Then, like a bolt from the blue, came Marcus Garvey, a Jamaican journalist, preaching a doctrine of Negro manhood, a doctrine that the time had come when the Negro was sick and tired of the indirect leadership of white overlords, a doctrine that met with the unanimous response from the millions of Negroes the world over."[6]

It may be that Walrond's pro-Garvey articles were motivated by a feeling of gratitude to one who had given him a job and a prize. Or perhaps they were purely opportunistic. Or it may be that Walrond was still in the process of working out his ideas on race uplift and literary aesthetics. At any rate a certain confused ambivalence soon crept into his writings and this in turn merely presaged a seemingly clean break with Garveyism.

A mere two weeks after the appearance of his prize-winning essay Walrond asserted, in an editorial on "Art and Propaganda," that Afro-Americans would never write great literature, such as Maran's *Batouala*, until they could "purge" themselves of their emotions and "write along colorless, sectionless lines." Yet he confusingly thought that when Black writing arrived at that point it would be "straight from the shoulder, slashing, murdering, disembowelling!"[7] In another editorial on the very same page he defended Black folk from Mary White Ovington's observation that "Negroes are prone to look at all literature, especially when it is about them, in the light of propaganda." "It might be inartistic and all that," was Walrond's rejoinder, "but the Negro is obliged to be suspicious of white people...."

Thereafter, this confusion gave way to a definite drift into the anti-propaganda camp. He soon emerged as the only important *Negro World* voice consistently against propaganda. Within four months he was praising T.S. Stribling's *Birthright* - "It steers clear of propaganda. It is genuine tragedy.... Birthright is a supreme work of art. If negroes do not like it, that is all right; but for God's sake, let white people read it; let them read it!"[8]

At about this time (1922), Walrond began obtaining

regular access to major white publications. This fact only
served to hasten his departure from Garveyism. Writing in
Henry Ford's *Dearborn Independent*, he described
Dunbar as the ideal Black poet, one who depicted the life
of the folk while stopping short of propaganda. By way of
contrast with Dunbar, he cited the case of Charles Wadell
Chesnutt, for "Chesnutt not only did not interpret the
soul-movements of the Black race, as Dunbar did, but he
was - especially in 'The Marrow of Tradition' - a purpose
novelist, a propagandist. Indeed, Chesnutt, from his lofty
pedestal, saw the red monster of race prejudice in all its
sordid colors and leveled his javelin at it. It is regrettable
for there is not the slightest doubt that Chesnutt knew
how to write, and wrote trenchantly."9 Walrond also
projected a theme here which he would later return to in
the *Negro World* - that Alexander Pushkin of Russia,
Alexandre Dumas of France and some of the mulatto
writers of Latin America, were the best of Black writers.
They were best because they were "quite ignorant of such
a white elephant as the race question."10

Walrond's drift away from Garveyism also began to
infect the subject matter of his fiction. A week after
writing a sketch of a beautiful fictitious Japanese girl, he
published a short piece entitled "The Castle D'Or." The
heroine was a "beautiful queen of old" with "ivory-white
hands" and "nymph-like arms, soft, baby-pink arms." A
"vision of loveliness" was she.11 In the context of the
Negro World this was strange stuff indeed. The woman
question in particular was one on which Garveyites were
very sensitive.

At least one outraged reader's letter found its way into
the paper. Walrond's story, he said, seemed "at variance
with the aims and objects of the UNIA." "Should a queen
necessarily have 'white hands' or 'pink skin'?" he
enquired -"O shades of white mania! Mr. Editor, you are

under its 'hypnotic' spell.''[12] This correspondent also questioned Walrond's grammar. A reply was forthcoming on the grammar, but Walrond ignored the more fundamental question.

A year later, Walrond got himself into the same kind of trouble again. This time the occasion was a young writers' evening at the 135th Street library. Countee Cullen, Gwendolyn Bennett, Langston Hughes, Sadie Peterson and Augusta Savage all read poems. Schomburg and librarian Ernestine Rose were in attendance. Walrond read a short story based on a white man / Black woman theme. It did not go down well with some of those present.[13]

In between these two incidents Walrond continued unchecked on his downward slide. An innocuous article appeared in the *New Republic* in November 1922. But by early 1923, he was ready for another leap downwards. He chose an article in *Current History* for his first attack on Garvey. To be sure, he was even harder on DuBois in this article. In DuBois' writings he found "a stream of endless woe, the sorrow of a mulatto whose white blood hates and despises the Black blood in him." And he conceded that Garvey towered "head and shoulders" above both Robert Russa Moton of Tuskegee and DuBois. But he called Garvey an "American Emperor" and a megalomaniac, amazing words for a *Negro World* editor.[14]

All of this contrasted sharply with an article of a year earlier, wherein he had defended Garvey's insistence of one hundred percent loyalty from his well-educated subordinates. Garvey had been hurt too often by opportunists, Walrond had argued then. "Did they start to work with the idea of rendering service to the cause, of subordinating personal greed and power to the larger interests of the movement? No. To them affiliation with it meant a means to a very definite personal end."[15] This

sounded strangely like a prophecy of the course that
Walrond, even then, had already embarked on.

Prior to the *Current History* article, Walrond's co-
editors were supportive of his forays into the mainstream
journals of white America.[16] But with this article came the
first intimations of concern. Ferris, hitherto his staunchest
admirer, now rebuked him gently.[17] He was also immediately demoted from associate to contributing editor.
He was briefly reinstated to associate editor a few weeks
later but by August 1923, his name had disappeared from
the *Negro World* editorial credits for good. That month the
first of his several *Opportunity* stories appeared.

In 1925, Walrond fired a parting shot at Garvey from yet
another major white publication, *The Independent*. By
now he was mostly unrecognizable from the person who
had once helped edit the *Negro World*. He spoke
disparagingly of "the hordes of black peasants" who
worshipped Garvey; of the "fairy dream world" which he
created to compensate for the "beauty and grandeur that
are lacking in their drab, unorderly lives;" of the "old
white-haired negro [probably John Edward Bruce], a
veteran agitator" who Garvey made duke of Uganda; of
the "multitude of black stableboys, cooks and bottle
washers, scullions and jim-swingers" out of whom Garvey
had "fashioned the timber of the crack African Legion-
naires." He was no easier on the "sombre-faced maidens
from the French and Dutch and English colonies along the
Spanish Main" who joined the UNIA's Black Cross Nurses.

The paper which he had helped edit for almost two years
he called a "medium of violence" and the "most bitterly
racial newspaper published by negroes....the bourgeois
colored people of the United States are ashamed to be
seen with it."

Three years after he had proclaimed the attractiveness
of Garvey's message, he now could not fathom Garvey's
appeal. Garvey was on bail pending appeal of his mail

fraud conviction, but yet he seemed to be getting stronger all the time. "Through some divine mystery," Walrond sighed, "Garvey is the 'Moses' of the black masses. Instead of diminishing, his power is growing daily. It is one of the anomalies of the complex racial problem of the age."[18] Garvey lost his appeal a few weeks after this article appeared and there is no telling what the effect of this and similar articles may have been in prejudicing the case against him.

Walrond meanwhile went from strength, to strength. He became business manager of *Opportunity* and in 1926 his collection of short stories, *Tropic Death*, was published, only the second collection of the Harlem Renaissance. The first was Jean Toomer's *Cane*, and it would be the 1930s before any others appeared from a major publishing house. The United States for Walrond was now "our country."[19] Gone was the self-conscious West Indianness that had intruded into his *New Republic* article of 1922. He had arrived.

Garvey referred to Walrond's turnaround in passing in 1928. He included him along with Claude McKay, W.E.B. DuBois, Walter White, James Weldon Johnson and others guilty of prostituting their craft "under the advice of white publishers" to demean their race. But McKay was the real target for that particular attack.

For Walrond, the defection paid off, at least in the short run. Yet, like several of the other luminaries of the Harlem Renaissance, he faded fairly quickly into obscurity. Once the novelty of literary Black folk had worn off and the economic depression of the 1930s had set in, the white benefactors of the Walronds and Hurstons tended to turn to other amusements. People like Walrond had striven so hard and destroyed so much of their own institutions to get where they wanted to go - and yet, Walrond must on occasion have asked himself whether it was all worth it.

In the late 1930s, when Walrond and Garvey were both living in London, Walrond again contributed to a Garveyite publication, this time the *Black Man* magazine. Walrond was the second most frequent contributor, after Garvey himself. His articles dealt with literature and politics and included one short story. Unlike the stories of *Tropic Death*, which were set in and around the Caribbean, this one was set in Afro-America, around the theme of a Black man forced by racism to flee the South - the theme that Amy Jacques Garvey had utilized in the *Negro World*. There was a mellow, mature quality to Walrond's writing now, and he had grown more radical. There was even evidence of some flirtation with the rhetoric of socialism. In one respect, however, he had not changed. He still considered Pushkin the greatest writer of African descent.

Claude McKay was not as much of a defector as was Walrond. For he never really endorsed the Garvey Movement with anything remotely resembling the completeness of Walrond's apparent conversion. McKay was a freewheeling spirit who did not suffer easily the constraints of any kind of organizational or ideological discipline. For a time he called himself a communist, but nevertheless fell out with his fellow leftists at the *Liberator* magazine, for which he worked. He was intermittently at war with DuBois and the integrationists, and not without good reason. With Marcus Garvey and the UNIA he carried on a longstanding love / hate relationship.

McKay began writing for the *Negro World* very early. Several of his articles appeared in 1919 and 1920. Some of these, at least, were commissioned by Hubert H. Harrison, McKay's first friend among the Harlem intellectuals.[20] (Harrison's role as a discoverer and nurturer of Black talent was as important as it has been unacknowledged. In addition to the writers he exposed through his pioneering book review columns, he was among the first to actively seek out and promote McKay, J.A. Rogers, the South African Solomon Plaatje and, indeed, Marcus Garvey himself).

The *Negro World* was one of the first Afro-American publications to give McKay a hearing. Many of his articles were journalistic reports on the situation in England, where he was from late 1919 to 1921. McKay also provided Black Londoners with copies of the *Negro World* and other Afro-American publications.[21]

McKay, in his own erratic way, could be communist or non-communist, Black nationalist or integrationist, propagandist or anti-propagandist as the mood took him. He tried to convince the readers of his autobiography that "my social sentiments were strong, definite and radical, but... I kept them separate from my esthetic emotions."[22] Yet his sonnet, "If We Must Die," is the most powerful fusion of art and outrage that it is possible to find anywhere. And after the supreme defiance of "If We Must Die," he was able to turn around and accept the bowdlerization of that poem by the English publishers of his first post-Jamaican collection, *Spring in New Hampshire*. It took a white man, Frank Harris of *Pearson's Magazine*, to lecture him on his spinelessness in this regard. "You are a bloody traitor to your race, Sir!" thundered Harris - "A damned traitor to your own integrity."[23]

Garveyites loved McKay for the exquisite beauty of his verse. They loved him for his fighting poetry. They loathed him for his inconsistencies. For it seemed that McKay was just as likely to embarrass the race as he was to exalt it.

"If We Must Die" received a Garveyite endorsement practically from the moment it was written. McKay was employed at the time in a train dining car and he read the poem to his fellow waiters. One of these, a Garveyite, immediately encouraged him to read it at Liberty Hall. He knew that such excellent and race-conscious art would make McKay a hero there. McKay declined. "As I was not uplifted with his enthusiasm for the Garvey Movement," he recalled, "yet did not like to say so, I told him truthfully that I had no ambition to harangue a crowd." 24

Had McKay accepted the Liberty Hall invitation, the pressure on him to publish his sonnet in the *Negro World* would have been great. One cannot imagine Garvey and his editors passing up such an opportunity. This might even have counteracted to some extent the refusal of DuBois' *Crisis* and Boston's W.S.Braithwaite to publish his early work. But McKay gave it instead to the *Liberator*, "because of that magazine's high literary and social standard." 25

"If We Must Die" was frequently mentioned with approval by *Negro World* writers. An editorial against lynching borrowed its title. 26 In his enthusiastic review of McKay's *Harlem Shadows*, Walrond wrote, in his Walrond way, that "the one, next to 'If We Must Die', which will probably find a snug place in the enflamed breasts of the propagandists and the black proletariat, is 'Enslaved'." 27

McKay's not very long-lived flirtation with communism inevitably brought him into conflict with Garveyites. For Garvey's Black nationalism did not go down well with communists. And his success excited their jealousy. The result was many long battles between Garveyites, on the one hand, and communists and socialist groups on the other. 28 As early as 1919, there had appeared in the *Negro World* an exchange of letters between McKay and Ferris on the question of socialism. 29 As an unofficial delegate to the Fourth Congress of the Communist International in Moscow in 1922, McKay claimed to be a communist, a member of the Workers (Communist) Party

of the U.S.A. and a representative of the African Blood
Brotherhood (ABB).[30] The communist front ABB had
recently tried, unsuccessfully, to infiltrate the UNIA by
"boring from within."[31]

McKay's association with the white leftwing (later
outright communist) *Liberator* received frequent attention
from the *Negro World*, which affected an attitude of
scornful amusement. "Claude McKay, the Jamaican poet,
who is associate editor of the *Liberator*, will be dressed up
as an Ethiopian Prince," the paper announced in an item
on the Liberator Costume Ball.[32] Two months later,
McKay ran into serious problems when police raided
another *Liberator* party. The upholders of the law were
upset by the communist inspired interracial dancing which
took place. The *Negro World's* commentary on this affair
was a satirical gem. It was unsigned, but the style
sounded suspiciously like Garvey himself. The ponderous
headline set the scene for what was to follow - "Claude
McKay, Negro 'Constab' Editor, Cause of Disturbance -
Whites Object to His Dancing with White Woman at a Ball
- Advocate of Social Equality." The article continued,

> Claude McKay, Negro protege of Sir Sidney Olivier of
> England, who was discovered by the Ex-Colonial Governor
> as a Negro Constable or "Constab" of exceptional ability,
> and who has since won a name as a poet, is alleged to have
> been the cause of a terrible mix-up at a recent ball given by
> the *Liberator Magazine* of New York.
>
> The *Liberator* is a radical paper published in the interest of
> Socialism, and McKay is one of its editors, being the only
> Negro on the staff - the other editors are white.
>
> At the ball there were white guests, and it is alleged that
> Claude McKay delighted himself in dancing with one of
> the white women, to which Police Captain Howard ob-
> jected. Claude McKay is an advocate of social equality,
> and it is alleged that he delights to be in the company of

white ladies.

> We are very sorry to note the occurence, but happenings of
> this kind tend to show the impossibility of Negroes ever
> gaining social recognition among the whites. Such Negroes
> who preach the idea of social equality may well throw up
> their hands at the experience of McKay, who has, for some
> time, been nursed by white philanthropists as an ex-
> ceptional Negro genius.[33]

This article was part of an exchange, sometimes by the
two principals, sometimes by their allies and subordinates, which went on in a variety of publications, for
several months. McKay attacked Garvey in the *Liberator*
and DuBois reprinted much of this in the *Crisis*. One
"Nefertari" wrote the *Negro World* from London expressing her indignation at DuBois for reprinting McKay's
"vaporous and iniquitous outpourings". The *Jamaica
Times* also carried McKay's remarks. James O'Meally, a
Jamaican UNIA organizer, happened to be in the island at
the time and wrote a rejoinder which the paper refused to
publish in full, considering it too vituperative.[34]

In the midst of all this, McKay fell out with Michael
Gold, now *Liberator* co-executive editor. The *Negro World*
said that Gold accused McKay of "Negroizing" the
Liberator and alienating its white radical readership.[35] In
his autobiography, written several years later, McKay
claimed that Gold was a little too proletarian propagandist
for him - Gold wanted the *Liberator* to "become a popular
proletarian magazine, printing doggerels from lum-
berjacks and stevedores and true revelations from
chambermaids."[36]

The *Negro World* devoted an unsigned editorial to
McKay's latest predicament. This time around it was
sympathetic to McKay, for he seemed to have been the
victim of some radical racism. "Gold," said the paper,

is a radical with a bourgeois complex. Like a majority of his fellow radicals, he is a violent Socialist, Communist, Unionist, Social Communist, Communist Unionist and Internationalist. Following the anti-capitalist fad, he is interested in Russia, China and Corea, Africa, Asia and the Negro. In the ills of all these groups he takes a solid interest. Over sex and psycho-analysis, poetry and pragmatism, psychology and the future of society - over all these things, he'd sit and talk. A don't-give-a-damner, he is a trust hater, an open shop advocate, and free of prejudice of any sort.

Yet he objected to working side by side with a Negro....37

With McKay's departure from the United States this round of commentary subsided. In 1928, however, Garvey was moved to comment on the publication of McKay's best-selling novel, *Home to Harlem*. "Whenever authors of the Negro race write good literature for publication," Garvey lamented, "the white publishers refuse to publish it, but whenever the Negro is sufficiently known to attract attention he is advised to write in the way that the white man wants. That is just what has happened to Claude McKay. The time has come for us to boycott such Negro authors whom we may fairly designate as 'literary prostitutes.'"38

DuBois wrote a similar review in the June 1928 *Crisis*. By this time he had joined the propaganda school and for once the two men saw eye to eye on something. "McKay has set out to cater for that prurient demand on the part of white folk for a portrayal in Negroes of that utter licentiousness which conventional civilization holds white folk back from enjoying," DuBois argued, " ...if enjoyment it can be called.... This demand, as voiced by a number of New York publishers, McKay has certainly satisfied, and added much for good measure."39

A violent *New York Times* editorial commentary published on Garvey's death, provided McKay with an opportunity for a final, somewhat sympathetic assessment of the man's life and career. The *New York Times* had suggested that Garvey, "no more represented the Negro race in this country than Mr. Capone or Mr. Hauptmann the white race." McKay thought this "a strange and cryptic comparison to Negro readers, for although Marcus Garvey was a demagogue, he was not a common criminal, a bandit ambushing and blackmailing the unwary wealthy, or a kidnaper and murderer of babies. Garvey was no violater of the human spirit; he was more obsessed with the idea that the spirit of humanity should flower more universally."[40]

8

Garvey the Poet

BLACKMAN!
What Is In Thy Bosom? Pluck It
Out - Is It Genius, Is It Talent
For Something? Let's Have It.
                              -Marcus Garvey

Garvey was a prolific poet, but he was no poet. His
conventional verse, with some exceptions, tends to the
clumsy and pedestrian. Metre and rhyme are forced and
the structure is distinctly pre-twentieth century. Yet his
poetry is not without importance, for he was a man of
importance. He used poetry to expound his political ideas,
to document his struggles, to express his private
emotions. His poems provide an alternative glimpse into
his mind and his movement. That he wrote poetry at all
will be considered remarkable by some, for the notion of
Garvey as lacking in intellectual sensibilities dies hard in
certain quarters. One is almost reminded of Phillis
Wheatley, whose publishers thought it expedient to
append to her volume the testimony of Boston's "most
respectable characters," who did "assure the World, that
the Poems specified in the following Pages, were (as we
verily believe) written by Phillis," who had but lately
been "brought, an uncultivated Barbarian, from
Africa...." [1]

It was while he was imprisoned in Atlanta that Garvey
turned seriously to poetical writing. Like many a political
prisoner in other places and times, incarceration provided
him with an enforced "leisure" such as he had not known

for many years. "I was so busy for the seven years
preceding my conviction," he said on his release, "that I
was not able to open a book. I had a library of 18,000
books, and I had not even time to open one of them.... In
Atlanta I had a library of 2,000 books; and I had all the
time to read and reflect...." [2]

Negro World editor T. Thomas Fortune greeted
Garvey's first poetic submissions with an enthusiastic
editorial. He saw Garvey as uniquely qualified to write
poetry. According to Fortune, "Only those who have
suffered greatly or felt the ecstacies of joy in its highest
and purest form, are capable of reaching the depths in
poetic expression which affect and move great masses of
people." [3] Garvey was eminently qualified on both counts.

By this time Garvey was, of course, a very seasoned
writer of prose. His articles, pamphlets and books had
been appearing for many years and his prose was in-
finitely better than his poetry. [4] In the field of prose he was
forceful, though elegant and witty, and generally
possessed of a polish which seemed to bespeak wide
reading. Some of his prose, unencumbered as it was by
awkward attempts at versification, was actually more
poetic than his poetry. In the best traditions of Black
sermonizing, some of his speeches and essays betrayed a
feel for rhythm and cadence that fell upon the ears like
beautiful verse. Two of his prose essays in particular, are
still frequently recited at concerts. One is "African
Fundamentalism," which he is said to have considered his
most perfect piece of writing. The other is his "First
Message to the Negroes of the World from Atlanta
Prison," better known as "If I Die in Atlanta." [5] Garvey's
poetry and prose seemed to illustrate the dictum of the
sixteenth century British poet, Sir Philip Sidney, that
"One may be a poet without versing, and a versifier
without poetry."

The poetic quality of Garvey's prose can be illustrated very strikingly if rendered as free verse, as in the following extract from "If I Die in Atlanta" -

> After my enemies are satisfied,
> In life or death
> I shall come back to you
> To serve
> Even as I have served before.
> In life I shall be the same:
> In death I shall be a terror
> To the foes of Negro liberty.
> If death has power,
> Then count on me in death
> To be the real Marcus Garvey
> I would like to be.
> If I may come in an earthquake,
> Or a cyclone, or plague, or pestilence,
> Or as God would have me,
> Then be assured
> That I shall never desert you
> And make your enemies triumph over you.
> Would I not go to hell a million times
> For you?
> Would I not like Macbeth's ghost,
> Walk the earth forever
> For you?
> Would I not lose the whole world and eternity
> For you?
> Would I not cry forever
> Before the footstool of the Lord Omnipotent
> For you?
> Would I not die a million deaths
> For you?
> Then, why be sad?
> Cheer up, and be assured
> That if it takes a million years
> The sins of our enemies
> Shall visit the millionth generation
> Of those that hinder and oppress us.

* * *

If I die in Atlanta
My work shall then only begin,
But I shall live,
In the physical or spiritual
To see the day of Africa's glory.
When I am dead
Wrap the mantle
Of the Red, Black and Green
Around me,
For in the new life
I shall rise
With God's grace and blessing
To lead the millions
Up the heights of triumph
With the colors that you well know.
Look for me
In the whirlwind or the storm,
Look for me
All around you,
For, with God's grace,
I shall come
And bring with me
Countless millions of black slaves
Who have died in America and the West Indies
And the millions in Africa
To aid you in the fight
For Liberty, Freedom and Life.

The prose composition which, in this writer's experience, rivals "If I Die in Atlanta" as a popular subject of dramatic readings, is Martin Luther King's "I Have A Dream" speech. This oration was the highpoint of the 1963 March on Washington, intended to coincide with the hundredth anniversary of Abraham Lincoln's emancipation proclamation. The two works betray interesting similarities. It may be that the Reverend Dr. King was familiar with Garvey's essay. It may be that both men were simply tapping and tuning in to an ancient tradition of Black sermonizing, whose recurring symbols belong to the public domain.

Both works are litanies of past unrequited wrongs. In this respect King the integrationist sounded not too different from Garvey the nationalist - "One hundred years later," said King, "the Negro lives on a lonely island of poverty in the midst of a vast ocean of material prosperity.'" Both works are rich in imagery, although King's metaphors at times seem turgid, melodramatic and overdone, as witness - "This is no time to engage in the luxury of cooling off or to take the tranquilizing drug of gradualism.... Now is the time to rise from the dark and desolate valley of segregation to the sunlit path of racial justice. Now is the time to lift our nation from the quicksands of racial injustice to the solid rock of brotherhood.... This sweltering summer of the Negro's legitimate discontent will not pass until there is an invigorating autumn of freedom and equality."

King also repeated Garvey's "whirlwind" theme - "The whirlwinds of revolt will continue to shake the foundations of our nation...." The familiar imagery of hilltops and mountains also figures prominently in both works. Garvey would lead the race "Up the heights of triumph" and King would "let freedom ring from the prodigious hilltops of New Hampshire" and other assorted hilltops and mountains.

There is, after all is said and done, however, a fundamental difference between the two works. For Garvey is looking towards "the day of Africa's glory" when African peoples will be independent and strong. "Be assured," he says, "that I planted well the seed of Negro or Black nationalism which cannot be destroyed." The Rev. King, on the other hand, is dreaming of racial integration - "I have a dream that one day on the red hills of Georgia the sons of former slaves and the sons of former slaveowners

will be able to sit down together at the table of
brotherhood."[6] Both men were dreaming dreams, dreams
that might not come to pass in their lifetimes. But they
were dreaming different dreams. And the continuing
popularity of both compositions speaks alike to the two
differing ideological currents within the Black community
and to the reverence for The Word in the experience of
African peoples.

Garvey's formal poetry was published between 1927
and 1939, principally in the *Negro World* and his *Black
Man* magazine. Amy Jacques Garvey collected most of his
early poems into two volumes, *The Tragedy of White
Injustice* and *Selections from the Poetic Meditations of
Marcus Garvey*, both published in 1927. His *Universal
Negro Improvement Association Convention Hymns*
(Kingston, 1934), included further selections.

A few of Garvey's poems contained autobiographical
fragments. In "The Start" (1927) he revealed what is in
fact the way in which he embarked upon his lifetime career
of race organization -

> So find yourself in early age,
>   To know what you shall be in life;
> Then go and write on hist'ry's page
>   The vict'ries of your daily life.

Garvey's life work was dominated by an unusual
singleness of purpose. His penchant for political activity
was already evident during his early manhood and from
the day (1914) that he founded the UNIA in Jamaica to his
death in 1940, the organization never ceased to dominate
his life. This pattern was exemplified in the following
verse from "Those Who Know" (1935) -

> All life must be a useful plan,
>   That calls for daily, serious work -

> The work that wrings the best from man -
> The work that cowards often shirk.

Some of these autobiographical fragments dealt with specific problems encountered by Garvey and the UNIA. In his long poem, *The Tragedy of White Injustice* (1927), which a UNIA advertisement described as "An Epic of Rare Beauty, with an Historical Theme," he bemoaned the unhappy fate of the Black Star Line Steamship Corporation.[7]

> The white man controls cable and wireless,
> Connections by ships with force and duress:
> He keeps black races of the world apart,
> So to his schemes they may not be smart:
> "There shall be no Black Star Line Ships," he says,
> "For that will interfere with our crooked ways...."

Garvey's poetical notice of his tribulations included the press campaign to portray him as a buffoon and a clown. He observed, in *The Tragedy of White Injustice*, that

> In the vicious order of things today,
> The poor, suffering black man has no say....
> "If one should show his head as a leader,
> Whom we cannot use, the rest to pilfer,
> We shall discredit him before his own,
> And make of him a notorious clown.

In the same poem, Garvey attributed much of the press campaign against him to the fact that "Capitalists buy up all blank space / To advertise and hold the leading place." The average person, he argued, was unaware of how these sinister forces manipulated public opinion. It was for the "reformer" to counter this state of affairs, and that was not an easy task. In an obvious reference to his own experience, he warned that

> This isn't a smooth or very easy job,

> For, you, of your honor and name, they'll rob.

Nor would they stop at despoiling the reformer of his good name. Writing from prison, Garvey could authoritatively state that

> From banks they find out your real account,
> Then have you indicted on legal count:
> Large fees they charge, to have you surely broke,
> Then, to prison you go - what a sad joke!

And even Garvey's efforts to circumvent the hostile press by publishing his own newspaper were not free from harassment. The British, French and other colonial powers banned the *Negro World* in the West Indies, Africa and Latin America.[8] In *The Tragedy of White Injustice*, Garvey had these colonialist powers say,

> "We will keep from them the 'NEGRO WORLD'
> That no news they'll have of a flag unfurled;
> Should they smuggle copies in, and we fail,
> We will send the sly agents all to jail."
> This is the white man's plan across the sea.
> Isn't this wily and vicious as can be?

Garvey's problems with the press were of course not confined to the white press. In 1934, apparently stung by something from the pen of conservative Afro-American journalist, George S. Schulyer, he penned "George S. Schuyler Again," which contained the following lines -

> George S. Schuyler is a joke;
> His brain must be like sausage pork,
> Or he must be a "nutty" ass
> To bray at those he cannot pass....

Autobiographical fragments could on occasion recount more pleasant episodes. In "My Trip to the West Indies" (1937), Garvey expressed his appreciation to the en-

thusiastic West Indian crowds who flocked to his lectures.
He wrote,

> I ne'er shall joys of such a kind forget,
> As coming from those friends out there I met.

Family and friends were also extolled in Garvey's
poetry. "The Love Amie" (1927) was dedicated to his
wife, Amy Jacques Garvey. Despite the ups and downs of
race leadership, which had landed him in prison, the love
and understanding of his wife were the two good things
that he could confidently expect. And though the first
child of the marriage was not born until 1930, "Love's
Morning Star" of 1927 looked forward to this event -

> I've waited patiently for you,
>   And now you come to make me glad;
> I shall be ever good and true,
>   And be the dearest, sweetest dad.

"A Recitative Song!" of 1934 was dedicated to his second
son, Julius Winston Garvey. And one of Garvey's more
beautiful poems, "The Last Farewell" (1927) was a
requiem to an unnamed departed friend -

> Good-bye, my friend, in death we part,
>   To meet in realms more glorious:
> A void I feel deep in my heart,
>   For much there was of love in us:
> To see you go is awful pain,
>   For thou hast been a world to me;
> But we shall meet for good again,
>   To see the light that hallows thee.

All the main attributes of Garvey's philosophical and
ideological outlook can be found in his poems. Basic to his
outlook was a deep and ineradicable empathy with the
oppressed. In "The City Storm" (1927), a rare conscious
attempt at free verse, he expressed this in an unusual

manner. He first reflected on man's frailty in the face of the forces of nature. He observed,

> It was not the end of all time, nor
>   the hour for Gabriel's horn:
> It was atmospheric change, caused through
>   elemental moodiness,
> That sometimes make[s] us feel that our
>   sciences are but speculations,
> And the majesty of man, feeble, as
>   his finite intellect:
> Yet, there was a fear and trembling
>   as I observed it all around!

This set the stage for him to wonder how a human being, in all his obvious weakness, could find the "heart to enslave the rest of his fellowmen,/When conscience must tell him withal, we are in reality one?"

His feeling for the downtrodden received eloquent expression in "The Song of the Negro Maid" (1934) in which the unfortunate woman triumphs over her circumstances. She sings,

> The white man forced my head to bow,
> My chastity to treat with scorn;
> But I am queen of self, and now
> I feel as pure as I was born.

In *The Tragedy of White Injustice* Garvey contrasted the unequal justice meted out to a petty thief, on the one hand, and the rapacious capitalist, on the other -

> The common thief now steals a crust of bread,
> The law comes down upon his hungry head;
> The haughty land robber steals continents,
> With men, oil, gold, rubber and all contents.

The longest day had an end, however, for

Sooner or later each people take their stand
To fight against the strong, oppressive hand.

And this, Garvey assured us, "is God's plan."

Garvey's intolerance of oppression flowed from a strong religious sense. His poems are permeated with references to God and religion. His religion, however, was harnessed very securely to the struggle for racial emancipation. In a prose prayer from his *Universal Negro Improvement Association Convention Hymns*, this is demonstrated very effectively, in the following words -

> Almighty Saviour, whose heavy Cross was laid upon the stalwart shoulders of Simon the Cyrenian, a son of Ham, in that sad hour of Thine agony and mortal weakness, when the sons of Shem delivered Thee into the hands of the sons of Jepheth to be crucified, regard with Thy favour this race still struggling beneath the cross of injustice, oppression and wrong laid upon us by our persecutors. Strengthen us in our determination to free ourselves from the hands of our enemy; put down the mighty from their seat, and exalt Thou the humble and meek, through Thy mercies and merits who livest and reignest with the Father and the Holy Ghost, world without end.
>
> Amen

The title of the 1927 poem, "God in Man," expressed Garvey's idea that all persons had within them the divine-inspired potential to realize their full worth and free themselves from the shackles of oppression. In this poem Garvey told the oppressed,

Thou art the living force in part,
The Spirit of the Mighty I.

Garvey repeated this use of the pronoun "I" in speeches in Jamaica between 1928 and 1935 and he may perhaps be responsible for the unique use of that pronoun among persons of the Rastafarian faith, who in any event regard him as a prophet. "The White, Sinful Church" (1935), expressed his attitude to white Christianity, which he considered largely a perversion of Christ's teachings. In *The Tragedy of White Injustice*, he observed,

> With the Bible they go to foreign lands
> Taking Christ and stealth in different hands....

The idea of race first was central to Garvey's ideology and spoke to the need for Black people to put their own racial salvation above other concerns. Closely allied to race first was the need to instill pride in self. One way to do this was to rehabilitate the image of the Black woman who, during slavery, peonage and colonialism had often been an unwilling object of sexual abuse. Garvey placed himself squarely in the tradition of the *Negro World* poets when he discussed this unfortunate reality. The following passage from *The Tragedy of White Injustice* is reminiscent of "The Song of the Negro Maid" -

> Black women are raped by the lordly white
> In colonies the shame ne'er reaching light:
> In other countries abuses are given,
> Shocking to morality and God's Heaven.
> Hybrids and mongrels are the open result,
> Which the whites give us as shameful insult:
> How can they justify this? None can tell;
> Yet, crimes of the blacks are rung with a bell.

In "The Black Woman" (1927), he proclaimed his own idealized vision of the woman of the race - "Black queen of beauty, thou hast given color to the world!"

Involuntary race mixture arising from slavery and oppression could not be helped after the fact, but those Black persons who voluntarily continued this practice were likened by Garvey to traitors. In "Wanting to Desert" (1937) he told the following story -

A Negro who got rich did stray
  To claim he was not of the race,
But all the world could only say
  He was a fool and sore disgrace.

Race first for Garvey was not a racist position. It meant simply that the race would have to mobilize its political, economic and cultural resources to free itself from bondage and obtain equality with other peoples. In *The Tragedy of White Injustice* he showed that while Black folk would have to struggle relentlessly against white domination and oppression, such a struggle could not be based on simplistic considerations of race only. He addressed himself thus to the white race -

Blacks do not hate you because you are white;
We believe in giving to all men right....
Let justice prevail, at home and abroad;
Cease over the weak your burdens to lord....

Race first also meant that Black people would have to be self-reliant. The race would have to assume primary responsibility for freeing itself and this would mean hard work and discipline. Garvey was no friend of lazy Black folk who could not be moved to stir for themselves. In "Get Up And Work" (1934), he chided the race -

The Negro sits and pines all day:
His opportunities slip away....

Titles of other poems urged his followers to "Be King of Circumstances" (1935), and to "Have Faith in Self" (1927). In "Get Up and Go!" (1936), Garvey aggressively showed the way to self-reliance -

Please clear the way and let me pass,
If you intend to give up here....

The ultimate political objective for Garvey was
nationhood for Black people. During the UNIA's peak
period of the 1920s, this question was particularly acute.
The European scramble for Africa of the preceding half
century left Ethiopia and Liberia as the only remaining
independent nations on the African continent. Even Haiti
in the West Indies had been invaded and occupied by the
United States in 1915. Garvey's energies were therefore
largely directed at facilitating nationalist struggles
everywhere. A strong nation for the race was essential. In
The Tragedy of White Injustice he declared that,

> Each race should be proud and stick to its own,
> And the best of what they are should be shown;
> This is no shallow song of hate to sing,
> But over Blacks there should be no white king.
> Every man on his own foothold should stand,
> Claiming a nation and a Fatherland!
> White, Yellow and Black should make their own laws,
> And force no one-sided justice with flaws.

The most logical place for a strong, central Black nation
would be Africa.[9] The UNIA established branches in
several African countries and Garvey made an un-
successful effort to build a base in Liberia. His long range
Pan-African vision was, however, expressed in the title of
a 1927 poem - "Hail! United States of Africa!" His Pan-
Africanism also, of course, encompassed co-operation
among Black people the world over. In "The Mighty
Three" (1934), he wrote,

> Three ancient Negroes gathered at the old Cross Roads,
> An African, West Indian and American;
> They talked of separation days of slavery,
> And pledged ne'er more divided be in world of bravery.

Not surprisingly, many of Garvey's later poems were

devoted to the Italian aggression against Ethiopia, which
began in 1935. Some of his most vitriolic verses were
reserved for Benito Mussolini, the Italian fascist leader. In
"The White Man - Spirit of Mussolini" (1936) he portrayed Mussolini as an embodiment of the whole history of
white imperialism and genocide. In "The Devil In
Mussolini" (1936), he called the Italian "This devil in mad
human form...." In "The Smell of Mussolini" (1936), he
promised that Africans would avenge themselves on
Rome, if it took a thousand years.

Garvey's whole ideological outlook was rooted in a deep
appreciation for Black history. In "Far Up The Heights"
(1937), he took issue with those who tried to deny the
African's place in history -

> Who said the Black Man never lived
> In History with his deeds most great?

Nineteenth and early twentieth century Black historians
were preoccupied with the exploits of the ancient Africans
in Egypt and Nubia, who led the world in civilization and
who in turn helped civilize Greece and Europe. Garvey
shared this preoccupation, for it was a potent weapon in
the struggle against the pseudo-scientific racists who
claimed that Africans had not known civilization before the
arrival of Europeans in their midst in comparativley recent
times. "The Black Woman," in an obvious reference to
classical Greek and biblical sources, informed the women
of the race that,

> When Africa stood at the head of the elder nations,
> The Gods used to travel from foreign lands to look at thee....
> Thy transcendent marvelous beauty made the whole world mad,
> Bringing Solomon to tears as he viewed thy comeliness....

The Tragedy of White Injustice illustrated Garvey's wider political use of history. It recounted the glorious deeds of African soldiers from the dawn of history. Again drawing on classical sources, he informed us that,

> The Black Archers of Ethiopia stood
> At Marathon, proving their stern manhood....

Similar feats were performed through the ages,

> So down the line of history we come,
> Black, courtly, courageous and handsome.

In addition to thus instilling pride, the poem recounted the history of European colonialist expansion, and the genocide and forced racial mixture that it brought in its wake. This led to a demand for liberty for the oppressed -

> All that the other races want, I see,
> Is the right to liberty and be free;
> This the selfish white man doesn't want to give;
> He alone, he thinks, has the right to live.

Finally, there came a call to arms, coupled with a prediction of victory -

> Out of the clear of God's Eternity
> Shall rise a kingdom of Black Fraternity;
> There shall be conquests o'er militant forces;
> For as man proposes, God disposes.
> Signs of retribution are on every hand:
> Be ready, black man, like Gideon's band.
> They may scoff and mock at you today,
> But get you ready for the awful fray.

> In the fair movement of God's Abounding Grace
> There is a promised hope for the Negro race;
> In the sublimest truth of prophecy,
> God is to raise them to earthly majesty.

> Princes shall come out of Egypt so grand,
> The noble black man's home and Motherland....

And like many of the world's other great reformers and revolutionaries, Garvey looked forward to the birth of a new person, once freedom was regained -

> A brand new world of justice is to be!
> "You shall be a true brother unto me!"

9

Conclusion

The Garvey Movement in general, and the *Negro World* in particular, played a role in providing a potential infrastructure for the Harlem Renaissance, which needs take second place to none. The *Negro World* reached many more people every month than the *Crisis*, *Opportunity* and *Messenger* combined. At its peak circulation of 200,000 it reached more people weekly than those three reached in a month.

It pioneered a regular, fully developed book review section. Its literary competition of 1921 significantly predated those of *Opportunity* and the *Crisis*.

The UNIA Dramatic Club was earlier in the field than DuBois' Krigwa Players Little Negro Theatre. The *Negro World* published a truly massive amount of poems, stories and criticism weekly. It had a group of editors who were the intellectual equals of any anywhere - Harrison, Ferris, Bruce, Walrond, the Postons, Fortune and Garvey himself as managing editor - here was a combination that was superior to most and inferior to none. The regular contributors were every bit as impressive as the editors, including as they did Ali, Schomburg, Woodson, Rogers, Maloney and Lucian B. Watkins. It comes as no surprise to find that Alain Locke's much praised anthology on *The New Negro* (1925) included several *Negro World* "graduates" among its contributors - McKay, Hurston, Walrond, Rogers, Schomburg and W.A. Domingo (a *Negro World* editor in 1919), had all been intimately connected with Garvey's organ. Locke himself had published in the *Negro World*.

Yet it can be argued that the potential infrastructure that the Garvey Movement helped build for the Harlem Renaissance remained, to some extent at least, just that - a potential infrastructure. It was an infrastructure composed of a large international Black community united by the Garvey aesthetic. What the Harlem Renaissance proper too often provided was a group of talented Black artists writing or performing under the direction of white mentors and publishers and largely for white audiences. There were no large publishing houses satisfying the special needs of the *Negro World* readership, despite their numbers. If Garvey had been left alone perhaps he would have filled this need. But from his conviction in 1923, the UNIA was too preoccupied trying to keep him out of jail. From 1925 to 1927, he was *in* jail. And in 1927 he was deported.

Between Garvey's potential infrastructure, then, and the superstructure of the Harlem Renaissance, there remained a missing link. It is not correct to say (even as some *Negro World* contributors said) that there was no sufficient Black market for Black literature. The *Negro World* proved that such a market existed - and it was a large market. But the Harlem Renaissance superstructure was by and large not sufficiently addressing that market. The superstructure was largely hijacked away from that market by the lure of white acceptance. In vain did Harrison and Garvey (and eventually DuBois) complain of the disdain of big publishers towards the Black reading public and the unreasonable demands they made on their Black authors. In vain, because there were no alternative publishing houses of equal power and stature. So Garvey's potential infrastructure could do nothing but stand helplessly by as one after another of the gifted Black writers either got unhitched from it or studiously avoided it altogether.

The dependence of the more successful Harlem

Renaissance writers on white publishers and a white
audience left them in a most vulnerable position. For one
thing, those Black writers who had early on touched base
with the potential infrastructure felt the need, once
mainstream acceptance came within reach, to burn the
bridges they had crossed. Walrond and Hurston exemplified this most painfully.

Such behavior, however, served only to activate an
inexorable dialectic. For Black literary success gained at
the expense of the larger Black community contained
within it the seeds of its own destruction. Hurston and
Walrond on one extreme, and Rogers and Woodson on the
other, illustrated this point.

Neither Rogers nor Woodson made the break with their
community and neither made it to the publishing big time.
But both remained perennial favorites in their own
communities, year in and year out, and irrespective of
whatever transient fads may have gripped the larger world
outside. Walrond and Hurston, on the other hand, were
largely forgotten for decades (once the big publishers lost
interest in them) until they were reprinted in the 1960s
and 1970s.

Alain Locke, always more clear-headed than most of his
Renaissance protégés, could by 1929 plainly see this
danger as it lurked in ambush for the Walronds and
Hurstons. He saw the Harlem Renaissance for the
transient fad that it was - a fad propelled largely by a white
bohemian desire for the sensual and the exotic. Locke
knew that this was no basis upon which to build a people's
literature. "The proportions [of the Renaissance]," he
wrote, "show the typical curve of a major American fad,
and to a certain extent, this indeed it is." He continued,
"We shall not fully realize it until the inevitable reaction
comes; when as the popular interest flags, the movement
will lose thousands of supporters who are now under its
spell, but who tomorrow would be equally hypnotized by

the next craze." If anybody knew the inner realities of the Harlem Renaissance it had to be Locke, for he had been its mentor for a long time. But now he sadly admitted that "to win a hearing, much exploitation has had to be tolerated. There is as much spiritual bondage in these things as there ever was material bondage in slavery." All he could do at this stage was wistfully hope that out of the ashes of the Harlem Renaissance there would arise a more durable Black literature, one with firmer roots in its own community.[1] Garvey had provided the infrastructure for such a literature, but Locke's protégés had chosen not to see it.

Locke's observations found a belated and pathetic echo in Claude McKay, who eventually discovered, with the benefit of much hard hindsight, that "The Harlem Renaissance movement of the artistic '20's was really inspired and kept alive by the interest and presence of white bohemians. It faded out when they became tired of the new plaything."[2]

Garvey himself, in a historically most unusual way, became the literary and artistic symbol par excellence of both major tendencies within the Black cultural world of the 1920s and 1930s. Those who subscribed to his aesthetic showered him with poetic praise. He was the single most popular subject of *Negro World* poetry. Some, like Ethel Trew Dunlap, wrote not one but several poems in his honor. Some of these poems were set to music and Arnold Ford composed the Garvey hymn, "God Bless Our President." Not even in prayer could the creative expression of pro-Garvey sentiment suffer restraint. From South Africa to Cincinnati, Garvey made his way into the religious expression of Black people.[3]

In music and drama too, Garvey recurred as a noble theme. The photographs of Van Der Zee and the sculpture of Augusta Savage added visual supplement to this riot of positive artistic portrayal. Garvey even loomed heroic in *The Flaming Sword*, a long novel by the notorious

Afrophobe, Thomas Dixon. However much he disliked
Black folk, Dixon could find no fault with one who seemed
to manifest no interest in generalized social intermingling
between the races.[4]

This artistic fascination with Garvey did not fade away
after his deportation from the United States in 1927 or
even after his death in 1940. But with the Black Power
movement of the 1960s, coupled with the elevation of
Garvey to national hero of Jamaica in 1964, it again
assumed vast proportions. And although Black Power
subsided in the 1970s, the Garvey revival has continued to
grow. The Jamaican reggae singers of the 1980s now take
the place of the *Negro World* poets of the 1920s. Garvey is
an ever repeated theme in their lyrics. He has also begun
to make his way into the calypsoes of Trinidad.

All over the Caribbean and Afro-America there has
recently taken place what can only be described as an
explosion of popular, often anonymous, Garvey-inspired
artwork. Street murals, posters, silk-screenings and
buttons of all description, paintings, here and there a
poem, at least one novel[5] - and the list keeps growing. It is
only a matter of time before somebody attempts a serious
film on the life and work of Marcus Garvey. Some of Afro-
America's best known artists have also joined the street
artists and the poster makers in building works around
Garvey's red, black and green.[6]

The elevation of Garvey to the position of positive
literary and artistic symbol did not go unchallenged in his
own time. Those who disputed the Garvey aesthetic made
a determined effort to do the reverse - to portray Garvey as
a buffoon, criminal and lunatic. Zora Neale Hurston sent a
copy of her anti-Garvey story to Carl Van Vechten and he
must have liked it. For his *Nigger Heaven* took a negative
view of Garvey, though not as wittily so as Hurston's story
had done. Wallace Thurman and Willard Jourdan Rapp's
Jeremiah the Magnificent did not get off the ground,

though its intent was the same. Eric Walrond made his contribution, via literary criticism. Theodore Ward's off-Broadway play, *Big White Fog* (1940) took a somewhat unsympathetic view of Garvey. And it was inevitable that someone would sooner or later compare Garvey to the buffoonish Emperor Jones. James Weldon Johnson of the NAACP obliged. As far as he was concerned, the Emperor Jones was but a modest fool compared to Garvey. Within a brief ten years, Johnson argued, "a Black West Indian, here in the United States, in the twentieth century, had actually played an imperial role such as Eugene O'Neill never imagined in his *Emperor Jones*."[7]

The most elaborate effort to build a work of fiction around a negative image of Garvey came, not unnaturally, from W.E.B. DuBois. Alain Locke, reviewing DuBois' 1928 novel, *Dark Princess*, thought he could discern therein "perhaps a thinly varnished Garvey."[8] Locke was absolutely correct.

Anyone familiar with DuBois' anti-Garvey utterances would have recognized the fictitious Garvey of *Dark Princess*. DuBois had long characterized Liberty Hall as a "low, rambling basement of brick and rough stone." He had long insisted on seeing in the UNIA only an alien movement not representative of Afro-Americans. He had described Garvey, in a major white magazine, as a "little, fat black man, ugly, but with intelligent eyes and big head...."[9] All of this and more was repeated under the guise of fiction in *Dark Princess*.

Garvey was transformed into Mr. Perigua, "a thin, yellow man of middle size," but his physical features were foisted onto Perigua's sergeant-at-arms, "a short, fat, black man" given to "intense declamation." Perigua's offices were on 135th Street in Harlem, the same as Garvey's and every bit as run-down as DuBois' vision of Liberty Hall. One approached them via "an ill-kept hall

and up dirty and creaking stairs, half-lighted...."
Perigua's followers were congregated in a room "hot with
a mélange of smoke, bad air, voices and gesticulations."
They seemed often "on the point of blows, but blows
never came." All of this puzzled the character Matthew,
"until he caught their broad a's and curious singing lilt of
phrase. He realized that all or nearly all were West
Indians.... They were to him singular, foreign and funny."

Perigua's followers seemed to love him very much. For
without much provocation they suddenly broke into "a
song with some undistinguishable rhyme on 'Perigua
forever' "- undoubtedly DuBois' caricature of "God Bless
Our President."

Matthew's overall opinion of Perigua was a synopsis of
DuBois' anti-Garvey statements from the *Crisis* and
elsewhere. "This man was no leader," he thought, "he
was too theatrical.... Matthew had at first thought him an
egotistic fool. But Perigua was no fool. He next put him
down as an ignorant fanatic - but he was not ignorant. He
was well read, spoke French and Spanish, read German,
and knew the politics of the civilized world and current
events surprisingly well. Was he insane? In no ordinary
sense of the word; wild, irresponsible, impulsive, but with
brain and nerves that worked clearly and promptly." [10]

Perigua was DuBois' answer to the Emperor Jones, a
"thinly varnished" DuBoisian Garvey indeed. DuBois had
by this time converted to the propaganda school and this
was propaganda with a vengeance. In the very year of his
novel's publication, he had assailed Claude McKay for
pandering to the "prurient demand on the part of white
folk" for the depiction of decadence and licentiousness in
Black literature. Yet he seemed nearly as guilty as McKay
of all this. Nor did he neglect the licentious side of
Perigua, whose "scrawny woman, half-dressed" was
made to intrude, for no apparent reason, into the

narrative.[11] DuBois' Matthew, by way of aside, seems to have been borrowed wholesale from J.A. Rogers' *From Superman to Man*. Matthew, like Rogers' Dixon, was a Pullman porter who had interrupted his university studies for world travel.[12]

Garvey's own personal involvement in building his potential infrastructure was as immense as could be expected from a busy political leader and one, moreover, who was under constant pressure from all manner of adversaries. His interest in literature and the arts predated the UNIA, and went back to his formative years in Jamaica. He himself was the first literary editor of the *Negro World* (and he never ceased to be its managing editor). It was he who laid down the political line upon which the Garvey aesthetic was built.

This ultimately political underpinning of all criticism, this Garvey aesthetic, this Black aesthetic 1920s style, provided the Garveyites with a tool for artistic analysis. It was a constant. It never changed. It could be applied with equal effect to poetry, drama, fiction, music or art or anything else. Did the piece of work contribute positively to the race's knowledge of itself? - to the way in which it was perceived by other races? Or, alternatively, did the work at least not demean the race, not hold it up to ridicule? Was it technically proficient? Or, if not, then did it at least represent a creditable tentative effort worthy of encouragement? Was its plot or theme consistent with the notions of race first, self-reliance, and nationhood? These are the questions that can be deduced from the artistic writings of the Garveyite group.

The Garvey writers were of course human, and there are as many opinions as there are people. So it was inevitable that the same tool of analysis, applied to the same work, would occasionally yield different results in the perceptions of different people. Thus Garvey, Ferris and the lady from Cambridge could attack *Emperor Jones* but Harrison could find something worthwhile in it.

These were exceptions that proved the rule. On the whole there was a remarkable consistency of outlook, considering the large number of critics and the span of time involved. The Garvey aesthetic could be seen in his 1915 praise for Edward Wilmot Blyden as one who had "done so much to retrieve the lost prestige of the race, and to undo the selfishness of alien historians and their history which has said so little and painted us so unfairly."[13] It could equally be seen in Harrison's review of J.A. Rogers' work in the 1920s or in Garvey's denunciations of Robeson's films in 1939.

It was the Garvey aesthetic that provided the essential difference between Garvey's potential infrastructure and the superstructure of the mainstream writers. The wealthy dilettantes who patronized the Renaissance loved exotic Harlem and genial Claude McKay and witty Zora Neale Hurston and jazz and speakeasies and Negro melodies and brown-skinned chorus lines; but they could not love Garvey. Garvey was not out to entertain anybody.

Notes

Chapter 1: Garvey, Black Arts, Harlem Renaissance

1. For exact location of branches see Tony Martin, *Race First: The Ideological and Organizational Struggles of Marcus Garvey and the Universal Negro Improvement Association* (Westport, Conn.: Greenwood Press, 1976), pp.15, 16, 361-73.

2. R.N. Murray, ed., *J.J. Mills - His Own Account of His Life and Times* (Kingston: Collins and Sangster, 1969), pp. 108,   109.

3. Martin, *Race First*, pp. 91-100.

4. Tony Martin, *Amy Ashwood Garvey: Pan-Africanist, Feminist and Wife No. 1* (forthcoming).

5. Martin, *Race First*, pp. 6,   7, 280-83.

6. Alain Locke, *The New Negro* (New York: Atheneum, 1969, first published 1925), p. 49.

7. See Martin, *Race First*, pp. 314-333.

8. Quoted in *Negro World*, May 13, 1922.

9. Charles S. Johnson in Alain Locke, ed., *The New Negro* (New York: Atheneum, 1969, first published 1925), pp. 295-6.

10. The African Orthodox Church was closely connected with, though not officially a part of the UNIA. See Martin, *Race First*, pp. 71-73.

11. Claude McKay, *Harlem: Negro Metropolis* (New York: Dutton, 1940), p. 177.

Chapter 2: The Garvey Aesthetic

1. *Negro World*, September 29, 1928, quoted in Martin, *Race First*, p. 26.

2. *Negro World*, December 2, 1922.

3. Amy Jacques Garvey, ed., *Philosophy and Opinions of Marcus Garvey, II* (New York: Atheneum, 1969, first pub. 1923 and 1925), n.p.

4. *Negro World*, June 9, 1923.

5. Claude McKay, *A Long Way From Home* (New York: Harcourt, Brace and World, 1970, first pub. 1937), pp. 26, 27.

6. *Negro World*, September 29, 1928, quoted in Martin, *Race First*, p. 26.

7. See Chapter 6.

8. *Negro World*, March 26, 1921.

9. Ibid, July 30, 1921.

10. Ibid, June 20, July 11, 1931.

11. Ibid, August 21, 1920.

12. Ibid, July 7, 1923.

13. Ibid, July 31, 1920.

14. Ibid, March 31, 1923.

15. Ibid, April 15, 1922.

16. Ibid, September 29, 1928, quoted in Martin, *Race First*, p. 26.

17. Locke, ed., *The New Negro*, p. 167.

18. *The Dearborn Independent*, May 13, 1922.

19. *Time*, November 10, 1980, p. 77.

20. *Negro World*, October 7, 1922.

21. Martin, *Race First*, p. 26.

22. Reprinted in Addison Gayle, Jr., ed, *The Black Aesthetic* (Garden City, N.Y.: Anchor Books, 1972), p. 167.

23. *Negro World*, July 10, 1926.

24. Carl Van Vechten, *Nigger Heaven* (New York: Octagon Books, 1980, first pub. 1926), pp. 175, 176.

25. Alain Locke, ed., *The New Negro*, pp. 43,44.

26. Ibid, pp. 40, 41.

27. Ibid, pp. 43, 44.

28. Arnold Rampersad, *The Art and Imagination of W.E.B. DuBois* (Cambridge: Harvard University Press, 1976), p. 184.

29. Martin, *Race First*, pp. 309, 310.

30. *Negro World*, June 17, 1922.

31. Claude McKay, *A Long Way From Home* (New York: Harcourt, Brace and World, 1970, first pub. 1937), p. 28.

32. Claude McKay, *The Negroes In America*, ed. by Alan L. McLeod (Port Washington, N.Y.: Kennikat Press, 1979, first pub. ca. 1923), p. 73.

33. McKay, *A Long Way From Home*, p. 139.

34. *Negro World*, July 8, 1922.

35. Countee Cullen, *Caroling Dusk* (New York: Harper and Brothers , 1927), p. xiii.

36. In Locke, ed., *The New Negro*, p. 40.

37. James Weldon Johnson, *Black Manhattan* (New York: Atheneum, 1968, first pub. 1930), p. 267.

38. James Weldon Johnson, *The Book of American Negro Poetry* (New York: Harcourt, Brace and World, 1959, reprint of 1931 edition), pp. 5,6.

39. McKay, *A Long Way From Home*, p. 227.

Chapter 3: Garveyism and Literature

1. *Negro World*, April 29, 1922.

2. Ibid. Maloney did not mention DuBois and Garvey by name, but his allusions to them were clear enough.

3. Ibid. April 7, 1923.

4. Liberty Hall was the name given to the meeting places of UNIA locals. Each branch had its Liberty Hall, whether owned or rented.

5. *Negro World.*, January 19, 1924.

6. All three worked for the rival NAACP. The "Lunatic or Traitor" editorial is in the *Crisis*, May 1924, p. 8.

7. *Negro World*, May 10, 1924; Tony Martin, *Race First: The Ideological and Organizational Struggles of Marcus Garvey and the Universal Negro Improvement Association* (Westport, Conn.: Greenwood Press, 1976), pp. 302-304.

8. M.I. 1c to Foreign Office on "Negro Agitation," January 7, 1920, FO 371/4567, Foreign Office files, Public Record Office, London.

9. *Negro World*, September 16, October 14, 1922.

10. Ibid, November 18, 1922, April 28, 1923.

11. Ibid, April 22, 1922.

12. On Murray see Tony Martin, "Race Men, Bibliophiles and

Historians: The World of Robert M. Adger and The American Negro Historical Society of Philadelphia,'' in Wendy Ball and Tony Martin, *Rare Afro-Americana: A Reconstruction of the Adger Library* (Boston: G.K. Hall and Co., 1981), pp. 21-23; and Robert L. Harris, Jr., "Daniel Murray and *The Encyclopedia of the Colored Race*," *Phylon*, XXXII, 3, Fall 1976, pp. 270-282.

13. *Negro World*, May 6, 1922.

14. Ibid, July 2, 1921.

15. Ibid, July 15, April 29, January 21, 1922; Martin, *Race First*, pp. 24,25.

16. Martin, *Race First*, p. 285.

17. Martin, in Ball and Martin, *Rare Afro-Americana*, pp. 23,24.

18. Tony Martin, *The Pan-African Connection* (Cambridge, Mass.: Schenkman Pub. Co., 1983), p. 106.

19. *Negro World*, July 17, 1920.

20. Ibid, January 14, 1922.

21. Garvey's invitation is discussed, somewhat unsatisfactorily, in Alfred A. Moss, Jr., *The American Negro Academy* (Baton Rouge: Louisiana State University Press, 1981), pp. 276-277. Moss is not fully aware of the extent of Garveyite involvement in the American Negro Academy, or of the depth of Schomburg's Garveyite connections.

22. Martin, *Race First*, pp. 273-333.

23. Ibid, p. 331.

24. *Negro World*, December 10, 1921, January 7 and February 11, 1922, June 17, 1924.

25. Ibid, December 22, 1922.

26. Ibid, March 31, 1923.

27. Ibid, April 22, May 22, 1922.

28. Ibid, January 14, 1922.

29. Ibid, April 15, 1922.

30. Claude McKay, *A Long Way From Home* (New York: Harcourt, Brace and World, 1970, first published 1937), pp. 114,115.

31. *Negro World*, September 23, 1922.

32. Ibid, May 20, 1922.

33. Ibid, August 21, 1920.

34. Ibid, November 18, 1922.

35. Ibid, August 14, 1920.

36. Ibid, August 26, 1922.

37. Ibid, July 28, 1923, July 12, 1924. On the latter date the *Negro World* reprinted an *Opportunity* article.

38. Ibid, September 9, 1922.

39. Martin, *Race First*, pp. 291,292. For plagiarisms in DuBois' *Black Reconstruction in America* see Tony Martin, "Did W.E.B. DuBois Plagiarize?" *Afro-Americans in New York Life and History*, VI, 2, January 1982, pp. 51-53.

40. Martin, *The Pan-African Connection*, p. 106.

41. *Negro World*, November 18, 1922.

42. Ibid, April 23, 1921. Plaatje sold many copies of this and other works to UNIA members throughout North America.

43. James Weldon Johnson, *Black Manhattan* (New York: Atheneum, 1968, first pub. 1930), p. 277.

44. *Negro World*, December 17, 1921.

45. A few Walrond editorials, signed simply "E.D.W." actually appeared in the *Negro World* before the contest.

46. *Negro World*, December 17, 1921.

47. Martin, *Race First*, pp. 99, 162.

48. *Negro World*, December 31, 1921.

49. Ibid, January 28, 1922.

Chapter 4: Poetry for the People

1. *Negro World*, January 28, 1922.

2. Ibid, June 25, 1921.

3. Ibid, December 24, 1921.

4. *Ufahamu*, IX, 3, 1979-80, p. 139. Ho told the Afro-American leader of the 1960s, Robert Williams, that he attended UNIA meetings during a sojourn in New York as a young man. He contributed generously to the organization and was greatly impressed by Garvey - notes taken by author at lecture by Robert Williams in Boston.

5. Claude McKay, *The Negroes in America* (Port Washington, N.Y.: Kennikat Press, 1979, first pub. ca. 1923), p. 73.

6. Claude McKay, *A Long Way From Home* (New York: Harcourt, Brace and World, 1970, first pub. 1937), p. 11.

7. *Negro World*, April 16, 1921.

8. Tony Martin, *Race First: The Ideological and Organizational Struggles of Marcus Garvey and the Universal Negro Improvement Association* (Westport, Conn.: Greenwood Press, 1976), pp. 160-163.

9. *Negro World*, July 29, 1922.

10. Martin, *Race First*, pp. 280-283.

11. G. Herbert Renfro, *Life and Works of Phillis Wheatley* (Miami: Mnemosyne Publishing Company, 1969, first pub. 1916), p. 107.

12. Ibid, p. 80.

13. Ibid, p. 48.

14. Quoted in Tony Martin, *The Pan-African Connection* (Cambridge, Mass.: Schenkman Pub. Co., 1983), p.34.

15. Thomas Jefferson, *Notes on the State of Virginia* (New York: Norton, 1972, first pub. 1787), pp. 138,139. Jefferson was not impressed by Wheatley. He considered her poetry beneath the dignity of criticism - ibid, p. 140.

16. *Negro World*, July 1, 1922.

17. Ibid, July 16, 1921.

18. Countee Cullen, *Caroling Dusk* (New York: Harper and Bros, 1927), p. 182.

19. Ibid, October 22, 1921.

20. Ibid, September 3, 1921.

21. E.g., James McGirt, *The Triumphs of Ephraim* (1907).

22. *Negro World*, June 18, 1921.

23. Ibid, April 23, 1921.

24. Ibid, March 5, 1921.

25. Ibid, March 19, 1921.

26. Ibid, December 9, 1922.

27. "Lines to R.A. Bennett," ibid, August 5, 1922.

28. Ibid, September 23, 1922.

29. Ibid, October 14, 1922.

30. Reprinted in Richard Barksdale and Keneth Kinnamon, eds, *Black Writers of America* (New York: Macmillan, 1972), pp. 47,48.

31. *Negro World*, June 3, 1922.

32. Ibid, July 7, 1923.

33. Ibid, April 23, 1921.

34. Ibid, June 4, 1921.

35. Ibid, October 7, 1922.

36. Ibid, August 21, June 19, 1920.

37. Ibid, April 23, 1921.

38. Ibid, June 24, 1922.

39. Ibid, January 6, 1923.

40. Ibid, November 11, 1922.

41. Ibid, June 9, 1923.

42. *The African*, IV, 4, August 1946, p. 6; reprinted in J.R. Ralph Casimir, *Poesy* (Roseau, Dominica: 1948), p. 58.

43. Martin, *Race First*, p. 106 n. 31.

44. *Gold Coast Leader*, October 21, 1922.

45. *Negro World*, February 19, 1921.

46. Ibid, February 26, 1921.

47. Ibid, March 12, 1921.

48. Ibid, February 26, 1921.

49. Ibid, December 23, 1922.

50. Ibid, January 20, 1923.

51. Ibid, November 11, 1922.

52. Ibid, October 7, 1922.

53. Ibid, March 22, 1924.

54. Ibid; Martin, *Race First*, pp. 127-128.

55. *Negro World*, March 22, 1924.

56. Ibid, March 29, 1924.

57. Ibid, September 13, 1924.

58. Ibid, May 12, 1923.

59. Ibid, October 1, 1921.

60. Robert E. Hemenway, *Zora Neale Hurston* (Urbana: University of Illinois Press, 1977), pp. 24, 355-6. Robert Bone is equally unaware of Hurston's *Negro World* connections - *Down Home* (New York: G.P. Putnam's Sons, 1975), p.143 and bibliography.

61. The Zora Neale Hurston Collection at the Schomburg Center of the New York Public Library contains a few poems written in 1918 and 1919. There is no indication as to whether these were published or not.

62. Hemenway is somewhat confused about Hurston's whereabouts at this time (ca. 1922) and seems to think that she arrived in New York, where she had "no friends," in 1925 - *Zora Neale Hurston*, pp. 9, 18, 32, 33 n. 13, etc. The *Negro World* evidence suggests that she was spending a lot of time (perhaps living for a while at least), in Harlem in 1922.

63. Eric D. Walrond, "Visit to Arthur Schomburg's Library Brings Out Wealth of Historical Information," *Negro World*, April 22, 1922. Walrond says that "The young lady in our party is a Columbia student...." Hurston is the only lady mentioned in the article.

64. *Negro World*, April 15, 1922.

65. Ibid, April 1, 1922.

66. Ibid, April 8, 1922.

67. Ibid, April 15, 1922.

68. Typescript in the James Weldon Johnson Memorial Collection, Beinecke Rare Book and Manuscript Library, Yale University, Box 1, Folder 16. The manuscript bears no date but, from internal evidence, must have been written some time after August 1, 1924.

69. Carl Van Vechten, *Nigger Heaven* (New York: Octagon Books, 1980, first pub. 1926), pp. 31, 120.

70. *Negro World*, July 17, 1920.

71. Ibid, March 20, 1922. On Sekyi and Nkrumah see S.K.B. Asante, "Politics of Confrontation 1," *West Africa*, January 10, 1983, pp. 81-84.

72. *Negro World*, May 13, 1922.

73. Reprinted by Black Classic Press, Baltimore, 1978.

74. J.A. Rogers, *World's Great Men of Color, Vol. I* (New York: Collier, 1972, first pub. 1946), p. 9.

75. Harry Haywood, *Black Bolshevik* (Chicago: Liberator Press, 1978), pp. 100-101.

76. George Wells Parker to Contributing Editor, *Negro World*, n.d., Calendar of the J.E. Bruce Papers, Schomburg Center, New York, p. 331.

77. *Negro World*, September 29, 1923.

78. Haywood, *Black Bolshevik*, p. 101.

79. *Negro World*, July 1, 1922.

80. Ibid, June 4, 1921.

81. Ibid, March 11, 1922.

82. Ibid, October 7, 1922.

83. Ibid, April 22, 1922.

84. Ibid, May 20, 1922.

85. Ibid, May 18, 1929.

86. Ibid, July 22, 1922.

87. A. Mitchell Palmer, *Investigation Activities of the Department of Justice, Vol. XII of Senate Documents, No. 153, 66th Congress, 1st Session, 1919* (Washington, D.C.: Government Printing Office, 1919), p.163.

Chapter 5: Book Reviews

1. *Negro World*, March 4, 1922.

2. Ibid, March 11, 1922.

3. Ibid, January 7, 1928.

4. Ibid, March 11, 1922.

5. Hubert H. Harrison, *When Africa Awakes* (New York: Porro Press, 1920), p. 8.

6. Tony Martin, *Race First: The Ideological and Organizational Struggles of Marcus Garvey and the UNIA* (Westport, Conn.: Greenwood Press, 1976), pp.9, 92.

7. *Negro World*, January 7, 1928.

8. Ibid, March 11, 1922; March 4, 1922.

9. Ibid, May 6, 1922.

10. Ibid, July 22, 1922.

11. Martin, *Race First*, especially Chapter 11.

12. Ibid, p.274.

13. Ibid, pp. 287, 288, 303.

14. Ovington was almost totally silent on all this in her autobiographical *The Walls Came Tumbling Down* (New York: Harcourt, Brace & Co., 1947). But it seems (p.44) that she may have met Ferris many years before the UNIA was founded.

15. *Negro World*, March 18, 1922.

16. In Alain Locke, ed., *The New Negro* (New York: Atheneum, 1969, first pub. 1925), p. 34.

17. *Negro World*, March 11, 1922.

18. Ibid, December 15, 1923.

19. Ibid.

20. Ibid, March 4, 1922.

21. Ibid, October 28, 1922.

22. Ibid.

23. Ibid, March 11, 1922.

24. Ibid.

25. Ibid, September 23, 1922.

26. Ibid, March 25, 1922.

27. Ibid, July 1, 1922.

28. Ibid, July 29, 1922.

29. René Maran, *Batouala: A True Black Novel* (Washington, D.C.: Black Orpheus Press, 1972, English translation of 1938 "definitive edition." First pub. 1921), p. 9.

30. J.A. Rogers, *From "Superman" to Man* (New York: Helga M. Rogers, 1971, reprint), dust jacket.

31. *Negro World*, July 31, 1920.

32. Ibid, January 7, 1922.

33. Ibid, June 17, 1922.

34. Ibid, December 24, 1921.

35. Ibid, March 4, 1922.

36. Martin, *Race First*, p. 86.

37. *Negro World*, June 24, July 1, 1922.

38. Ibid, June 18, 1927.

39. Ibid, January 28, 1922.

40. Ibid, November 4, 1922.

41. Ibid; also November 11, 1922.

42. John E. Bruce to Woodson, January 17, 1923, Carter G. Woodson Papers, folder 77, box 5, Manuscript Division, Library of Congress.

43. T. Thomas Fortune to Woodson, December 21, 1923, Woodson Papers, folder 85, box 5.

44. Amy Jacques Garvey, *Garvey and Garveyism* (Kingston: A.J. Garvey, 1963), p. 68.

45. *Negro World*, June 30, 1923.

Chapter 6: Music, Drama, Art and Elocution

1. *Negro World*, June 19, 1920; August 26, 1922.

2. Ibid, August 19, 1922.

3. Ibid, June 10, 1922.

4. *Black Man*, August 27, 1929.

5. *Negro World*, August 21, 1920.

6. William Isles, *Our Leader - March Song* (New York: William Isles, 1921).

7. (New York: Seymour Music Publishing Company, 1927).

8. Marcus Garvey, *Universal Negro Improvement Assocation Convention Hymns* ([Kingston], 1934).

9. *Jamaica Times*, August 25, 1934.

10. *Negro World*, October 15, 1921; Tony Martin, *Race First: The Ideological and Organizational Struggles of Marcus Garvey and the UNIA* (Westport, Conn: Greenwood Press, 1976), p. 379.

11. Martin, *Race First*, p. 249. The comment was by Robert Minor of the Workers (Communist) Party.

12. William R. Scott, "Rabbi Arnold Ford's Back-to-Ethiopia Movement," *Pan-African Journal*, VIII, 2, Summer 1975, pp. 191-202; Martin, *Race First*, pp. 63 n.5, 75, 138.

13. Amy Jacques Garvey, ed, *The Philosophy and Opinions of Marcus Garvey, II* (New York: Atheneum, 1969, first pub. 1923 and 1925), p. 140.

14. *Negro World*, June 10, 1922.

15. Ibid, June 10, 17, 1922.

16. Ibid, September 9, 1922.

17. Ibid.

18. Ibid.

19. Ibid, November 5, 1921.

20. Ibid, November 19, 1921.

21. Martin, *Race First*, p. 25.

22. Tony Martin, *Amy Ashwood Garvey*, forthcoming.

23. *Negro World*, March 1, 1924.

24. Ibid, January 28, 1922.

25. Ibid, July 16, 1921.

26. John E. Bruce Papers, n.d., F 10, 8, Schomburg Center, New York Public Library.

27. Ibid, BD 10, D1.

28. *Negro World*, January 21, 1922.

29. Ibid, July 22, 1922.

30. Ibid, May 27, 1922.

31. *Black Man*, Late October 1935, pp. 10, 11.

32. Ibid, June 1939, n.p.

33. *Negro World*, October 17, 1933.

34. Ibid, November 9, 1929.

35. Paul Robeson, Jr., "Paul Robeson: Black Warrior," *Freedomways*, XI, 1, 1971, p. 26.

36. *Negro World*, April 22, 1922.

37. Martin, *Race First*, pp. 86-87.

38. See, e.g., Liliane DeCock and Reginald McGhee, eds, *James Van Der Zee* (Dobbs Ferry, New York: Morgan and Morgan, 1973).

39. Martin, *Race First*, pp. 100-103.

40. *Negro World*, September 3, 1921.

41. Claude McKay, *Harlem: Negro Metropolis* (New York: Dutton, 1940), pp. 152-3.

42. *Negro World*, March 18, 1922.

43. Ibid, August 21, 1920.

44. Ibid, October 14, 21, 1922.

45. Ibid, October 28, 1922.

46. Martin, *Race First*, pp. 260-61; *Negro World*, October 10, 1931.

47. Martin, *Race First*, p. 260.

Chapter 7: The Defectors - Eric Walrond and Claude McKay

1. E.g. James B. Yearwood of Panama, sometime UNIA secretary general; George O. Marke of Sierra Leone, supreme deputy potentate (deputy ceremonial head) of the UNIA; R.T. Poston from Detroit; John Sydney deBourg of Grenada and Trinidad, a UNIA commissioner.

2. Col. Hubert Fauntleroy Julian, "Black Eagle of the UNIA" and Captain Hugh Mulzac, Black Star Line veteran and captain of the *Booker T. Washington* during World War II.

3. Tony Martin, *Race First: The Ideological and Organizational*

Struggles of Marcus Garvey and the UNIA (Westport, Conn: Greenwood Press, 1976), p. 166.

4. *Negro World*, December 17, 1921.

5. Ibid, December 3, 1921.

6. Ibid, January 21, 1922.

7. Ibid, December 31, 1921.

8. Ibid, April 22, 1922.

9. Eric D. Walrond, "Developed and Undeveloped Negro Literature: Writers Desert Great Field of Folk-life for Propaganda," *The Dearborn Independent*, May 13, 1922, p. 12.

10. *Negro World*, October 21, 1922. This was an unsigned editorial but Ferris confirmed Walrond's authorship a week later.

11. Ibid., March 18, 1922.

12. Ibid, April 1, 1922.

13. Ibid, March 31, 1923.

14. Eric D. Walrond, "The New Negro Faces America," *Current History*, XVII, 5, February 1923, pp. 786, 787. The article was actually written in 1922.

15. *Negro World*, February 11, 1922.

16. Ibid, November 4, 18, 1922.

17. Ibid, February 3, 1923.

18. Eric D. Walrond, "Imperator Africanus - Marcus Garvey: Menace or Promise," *The Independent*, January 3, 1925, pp. 8-11.

19. Ibid.

20. Claude McKay, *A Long Way From Home* (New York: Harcourt, Brace and World, 1970, first pub. 1937), p. 55.

21. Ibid, p. 67; McKay also published in the *Crisis* and *Messenger* in 1919.

22. McKay, *A Long Way From Home*, p. 103.

23. Ibid, p. 98.

24. Ibid, p. 32.

25. Ibid, p. 34.

26. *Negro World*, June 17, 1922.

27. Ibid, May 6, 1922.

28. Martin, *Race First*, pp. 221-272.

29. Ibid, p. 260.

30. Claude McKay, *The Negroes in America*, edited by Alan L. McLeod (Port Washington, New York: Kennikat Press, 1979, first pub. ca. 1923), pp. xviii, 88-90. It is not clear as to whether McKay was telling the truth - ibid, pp. ix, x.

31. Martin, *Race First*, pp. 236-43.

32. *Negro World*, January 14, 1922.

33. Ibid, March 6, 1922.

34. Ibid, July 8, 1922, June 3, 1922.

35. Ibid, June 24, 1922.

36. McKay, *A Long Way From Home*, p. 139.

37. *Negro World*, July 1, 1922.

38. Ibid, September 29, 1928. Garvey sent this article in from France, which he was visiting at the time.

39. Both reviews are reprinted in Theodore G. Vincent, ed, *Voices*

of a Black Nation (San Francisco: Ramparts Press, 1973), pp. 357-60.

40. Claude McKay, *Harlem: Negro Metropolis* (New York: Dutton, 1940), p. 179.

Chapter 8: Garvey the Poet

1. G. Herbert Renfro, *Life and Works of Phillis Wheatley* (Miami: Mnemosyne, 1969, first pub. 1916), p. 17.

2. *Negro World*, January 7, 1928.

3. Ibid, October 22, 1927.

4. See Tony Martin, *Race First: The Ideological and Organizational Struggles of Marcus Garvey and the UNIA* (Westport, Conn: Greenwood Press, 1976), pp. 378-79, for a listing of Garvey's published works.

5. Amy Jacques Garvey, ed., *The Philosophy and Opinions of Marcus Garvey, II* (New York: Atheneum, 1969, first pub. 1923 and 1925), back matter and pp. 237-39.

6. Text of King's speech from "We Shall Overcome," (New York: Folkways Records, 1964).

7. See Martin, *Race First*, Chapter 8.

8. Ibid, pp. 93-100.

9. See Martin, *Race First*, Chapter 7.

Chapter 9: Conclusion

1. Alain Locke, "1928: A Retrospective Review," *Opportunity*, January 1929, reprinted in Theodore G. Vincent, ed., *Voices of a Black Nation* (San Francisco: Ramparts Press, 1973), pp. 353, 354.

2. Claude McKay, *A Long Way From Home*, quoted in John Henrik Clarke, "The Impact of Marcus Garvey on the Harlem Renaissance," *Marcus Garvey and the Vision of Africa* (New York:

Random House, 1974), p. 187.

3. Tony Martin, *Race First* (Westport, Conn: Greenwood Press, 1976), pp. 68, 69.

4. Ibid, pp. 352-354.

5. Gershom Williams, *A Hero for Jamaica: A Novel of the Living Legend of Marcus Garvey* (Jericho, New York: Exposition Press, 1973).

6. The red, black and green have become so pervasive now that a book on W.E.B. DuBois by a Marxist historian carried this symbol of Garvey's Black nationalism on its dust jacket - Herbert Aptheker, *Afro-American History: The Modern Era* (New York: Citadel Press, 1971). In the case of the better known artists (e.g. Geoffrey Holder, Romare Bearden, Akin Duro) Garvey himself does not necessarily appear in their paintings of red, black and green.

7. James Weldon Johnson, *Black Manhattan* (New York: Atheneum, 1968, first pub. 1930), p. 256.

8. Martin, *Race First*, p. 308.

9. Ibid, pp. 300, 297, 287.

10. W.E.B. DuBois, *Dark Princess* (Millwood, New York: Kraus-Thomson, 1974, first pub. 1928), pp. 43-46.

11. Ibid, p. 45.

12. Ibid.

13. Marcus Garvey, *A Talk With Afro-West Indians* (Kingston?, African Communities League, ca. 1915), quoted in Martin, *Race First*, pp. 68,69.

Bibliography

This study is the first to examine in any detail the literary and artistic aspects of the Garvey Movement. It has therefore, of necessity, leaned heavily on primary sources. The vast literary outpourings of the *Negro World* (1918-1933) have provided the foundation upon which this work is built. The select listing of secondary sources which follows contains those items found to be most helpful in supplementing the information provided in the *Negro World* and filling in the broad contours of the Harlem Renaissance. The archival sources, magazines and non-UNIA newspapers listed have also proved helpful.

Publications of the Garveys

Garvey, Amy Jacques. *Garvey and Garveyism.* Kingston: A.J. Garvey, 1963. Reprint. New York: Collier Books, 1970.

_____, ed. *Philosophy and Opinions of Marcus Garvey or Africa for the Africans.* 1923, 1925. Reprint. New York: Atheneum, 1969.

Garvey, Marcus, ed. *Black Man* (magazine).

_____, ed. *Negro World* (newspaper).

_____. *Selections From the Poetic Meditations of Marcus Garvey.* New York: Amy Jacques Garvey, 1927.

_____. *The Tragedy of White Injustice*. New York: Amy Jacques Garvey, 1927.

_____. *Universal Negro Improvement Association Convention Hymns* . [Kingston], 1934.

Manuscript and Archival Collections

John Edward Bruce Papers. Schomburg Center for Research in Black Culture, New York Public Library.

Zora Neale Hurston Collection. Schomburg Center for Research in Black Culture, New York Public Library.

James Weldon Johnson Memorial Collection. Beinecke Rare Book and Manuscript Library, Yale University.

Public Record Office. Colonial Office and Foreign Office Records, London, England.

Carter G. Woodson Papers. Manuscript Division, Library of Congress.

Non-UNIA Magazines and Newspapers

The African
Crisis
Gold Coast Leader
Messenger
Opportunity

Books and Articles

Ball, Wendy and Tony Martin. *Rare Afro-Americana: A Reconstruction of the Adger Library*. Boston: G.K. Hall,

1981.

Bone, Robert. *Down Home*. New York: G. P. Putnam's Sons, 1975.

Casimir, J.R. Ralph. *Poesy*. Roseau, Dominica: 1948.

Clarke, John Henrik, ed. *Marcus Garvey and the Vision of Africa*. New York: Random House, 1974.

Cullen, Countee. *Caroling Dusk*. New York: Harper and Bros., 1927.

DeCock, Liliane and Reginald McGhee, eds. *James Van Der Zee*. Dobbs Ferry, New York: Morgan and Morgan, 1973.

DuBois, W.E.B. *Dark Princess*. Millwood, N.Y.: Kraus-Thompson, 1974, first published 1928.

Gayle, Addison, Jr., ed. *The Black Aesthetic*. Garden City, N.Y.: Anchor Books, 1972.

Harrison, Hubert H. *When Africa Awakes*. New York: Porro Press, 1920.

Isles, William. *Our Leader - March Song*. New York: William Isles, 1921.

Johnson, Abby Arthur and Ronald Maberry Johnson. *Propaganda and Aesthetics: The Literary Politics of Afro-American Magazines in the 20th Century*. Amherst: University of Massachusetts Press, 1979.

Johnson, James Weldon. *Black Manhattan*. New York: Atheneum, 1968, first published 1930.

_____,ed. *The Book of American Negro Poetry*. New York: Harcourt, Brace and World, 1959, reprint of 1931 edition.

Kinnanon, Keneth and Richard Barksdale, eds. *Black Writers of America*. New York: Macmillan, 1972.

Locke, Alain, ed. *The New Negro*. New York: Atheneum, 1969, first published 1925.

Maran, René. *Batouala: A True Black Novel*. Washington, D.C.: Black Orpheus Press, 1972, first published 1921.

Martin, Tony. *Amy Ashwood Garvey: Pan-Africanist, Feminist and Wife No. 1*. Forthcoming, ca. 1984.

_____. "Did W.E.B. DuBois Plagiarize?" *Afro-Americans in New York Life and History*, VI, 2, January 1982.

_____. *The Pan-African Connection: From Slavery to Garvey and Beyond*. Cambridge, Mass.: Schenkman Pub. Co., 1983.

_____. *Race First: The Ideological and Organizational Struggles of Marcus Garvey and the Universal Negro Improvement Association*. Westport, Conn.: Greenwood Press, 1976.

_____, ed. *Garvey's Harlem Renaissance: A Literary Anthology of the Garvey Movement*. Forthcoming, ca. 1984.

_____, ed. *The Poetical Works of Marcus Garvey*. Dover, Mass.: The Majority Press, 1983.

Martin, Tony and Wendy Ball. *Rare Afro-Americana: A Reconstruction of the Adger Library*. Boston: G.K. Hall, 1981.

McKay, Claude. *A Long Way From Home*. New York: Harcourt, Brace and World, 1970, first published 1937.

_____. *Harlem: Negro Metropolis*. New York: Dutton, 1940.

_____. *The Negroes in America*. Edited by Alan C. McLeod. Fort Washington, N.Y.: Kennikat Press, 1979, first published ca. 1923.

Murray, R.N., ed. *J.J. Mills - His Own Account of His Life and Times*. Kingston: Collins and Sangster, 1969.

Palmer, A. Mitchell. *Investigation Activities of the Department of Justice, Vol. XII of Senate Documents, No. 153, 66th Congress, 1st Session, 1919*. Washington, D.C.: Government Printing Office, 1919.

Parker, George Wells. *Children of the Sun*. Baltimore:

Black Classic Press, 1978, first published 1918.

Rampersad, Arnold. *The Art and Imagination of W.E.B. DuBois*. Cambridge, Mass.: Harvard University Press, 1976.

Renfro, G. Herbert. *Life and Works of Phillis Wheatley*. Miami: Mnemosyne Pub. Co., 1969, first published 1916.

Robeson, Paul, Jr. "Paul Robeson: Black Warrior," *Freedomways*, XI, 1, 1971.

Rogers, J.A. *From "Superman" to Man*. New York: Helga M. Rogers, 1971, first published 1917.

_____. *World's Great Men of Color*, Vols. I and II. New York: Collier, 1972, first published 1946.

Van Vechten, Carl. *Nigger Heaven*. New York: Octagon Books, 1980, first published 1926.

Vincent, Theodore G., ed. *Voices of a Black Nation*. San Francisco: Ramparts Press, 1973.

Walrond, Eric D. "Dark Stars that Shine," *Classic*, February 1923.

_____. "Developed and Undeveloped Negro Literature: Writers Desert Great Field of Folk-Life for Propaganda,"*Dearborn Independent*, May 13, 1922.

_____. "Imperator Africanus - Marcus Garvey: Menace or Promise," *The Independent*, January 3, 1925.

_____. "On Being Black," *New Republic*, November 1, 1922.

_____. "The New Negro Faces America," *Current History*, XVII, 5, February 1923.

Williams, Gershom. *A Hero for Jamaica: A Novel of the Living Legend of Marcus Garvey*. Jericho, N.Y.: Exposition Press, 1973.

Index

Abyssinia, 54. *See also* Ethiopia
Africa, 13, 41, 78, 79, 95, 108,
    111, 113, 114, 115, 122, 139,
    152, 153
Africa and Orient Review, 38
African Abroad, The (Ferris), 80
African Blood Brotherhood, 135
"African Fundamentalism"
    (Garvey), 9
African National Congress, 39
African Orthodox Church, 7
Africa Times and Orient Review,
    3, 33, 38
Ajai, Sennebundo, 114-15
Ali, Dusé Mohamed, 3, 33, 36,
    38, 39, 78, 86, 91, 116, 117,
    119, 121, 156; foreign
    affairs specialist for *Negro
    World*, 33; photo, 82
A Long Way From Home
    (McKay), 101
American Negro Academy, 32,
    33-34, 42; Garveyite bloc in,
    33
Amos 'n' Andy, 12
Amsterdam News (New York),
    38
An African Convention, 113
Ashwood, Amy. *See* Garvey,
    Amy Ashwood
As Nature Leads (Rogers), 93,
    102.
Associated Publishers, 102
Association for the Study of
    Afro-American Life and
    History, 102

A Talk With Afro-West Indians
    (Garvey), 4
Bagnall, Robert W., 34
Band of the African Legion, 106
Barbados, 40, 44
Barnett, Ida Wells, 87
Batouala (Maran), 27, 30, 95-99,
    127
Belize, 44
Bell, William Service, 36
Bellegarde, Dantes, 64
Bennett, Gwendolyn, 35, 129
Bermuda, 44
Big White Fog (Ward), 161
Birth of a Nation (film), 11
Birkbeck College, 115
Birthright (Stribling), 27, 127
Black aesthetic, x, 8. *See also*
    Garvey aesthetic
Black Arts Movement, x, 1-7,
    43, 58; looks to Garvey for
    political inspiration, 2
Black Bourgeoisie (Frazier), 15
Black Cross Navigation and
    Trading Company, 72
Black Cross Nurses, 113, 130
Black History Month, 102
Black Jews, 108-09
Black Magic, 113
Blackman (1922), 30
Black Man (1933-39), 132, 144
Black nationalism, 21, 80; and
    Black Arts Movement, 1, 2,;
    advocated by UNIA, 2; and
    propaganda, 24; Garvey on,
    143

Black Star Line Steamship Corporation, 41, 47, 72, 77, 125, 145

Black Star Line Band, 106, 108, 113

Blyden, Edward Wilmot, 4, 117, 164

Boni and Liveright, 37, 92

Booker T. Washington University, 48

Book of American Negro Poetry, The (Johnson), 30, 68

Bradley, E.W., 108

Braithwaite, William Stanley, 18, 20, 68, 94, 100; rejects poetry by McKay, 10, 22, 134; on propaganda, 20-21; on McKay, 23

Brathwaite, Leonard L, 57-62, 88

Brawley, Benjamin, 100; *The Negro in Art and Literature,* 30

Brazil, 44

Bridges, William, 10

British Guiana, 40

British Honduras, 44

Broadside Press, 1

Brown Sugar, 113

Browne, Robert T., 32; in American Negro Academy, 33; *Mystery of Space,* 38

Bruce, Mrs. Florence, vi, 116

Bruce, John Edward, 5, 9, 26, 91, 100, 102, 104, 130, 156; funeral photo, vi; in Niagara Movement, 32; in Negro Library Association of New York City, 32; in American Negro Academy, 33; judge for *Negro World* literary contest, 40; poem to Garvey, 86; *Preaching vs. Practice,* 114; *Which One,* 114-15; photo, 82

Buck, Professor B.C., 30

Burns, Robert, 15, 20

Canada, 31, 44, 56

Cane (Toomer), 20, 131

Carnegie foundation, 102

Carpentier, Georges, 64

Carroll, Lewis, 93

Casimir, J.R. Ralph, 31, 64-65, 86, 89; *Poesy: An Anthology of Dominica Verse, The Negro Speaks, Farewell (and Other Poems), Black Man, Listen! and Other Poems,* 65

Central African Republic, 95

Century Magazine, 35

Challenge, 10

Champion magazine, 4

Chesnutt, Charles Wadell, 128

Children of the Sun (Parker), 80

China, 110

Cockburn, Captain Joshua, 125

Coleridge-Taylor, Samuel; *Twenty-Four Negro Melodies,* 111

Collins, Carita Owens, 90

Colombia, 44

Columbia University, 35

Coming Home to Africa, 114

Communist International, 134

Coppin, Bishop Levi J., 38

Corbi, Mrs. William A., 11-12

Costa Rica, 3

Creighton University, 80

Crisis, x, 18, 25, 28, 32, 35, 38, 39, 91, 134, 136, 137, 156, 162; rejects McKay's poetry, 10; attitude to aspiring

writers, 26
Cromwell, John Wesley, 42
Crummell, Alexander, 32, 117
Cuba, 32, 44, 57
Cullen, Countee, 23, 35, 51-52, 129
Current History, 129
Cushite, The (Perry), 31

Daily Negro Times, 104, 121
Dali, Salvador, 17
Davis, Henrietta Vinton, 33, 120
Day, William Howard, 117
Dearborn Independent, 16, 128
Detroit Contender, 71
Dill, Augustus Granville, 32, 35
Dixon, Thomas, 17; *The Flaming Sword*, 160
Domingo, W.A., 156
Dominica, 31, 44, 64, 86, 89
Douglass, Frederick, 117, 120
DuBois, W. E. B., 18, 24, 29, 33, 91, 100, 117, 126, 129, 131, 132, 156, 157; read by Garvey, 4; *Crisis* rejects McKay poetry, 10, 134; on propaganda, 21; criticized by *Negro World*, 22; attitude to aspiring writers, 26; "Lunatic or a Traitor," 28; and Niagara Movement, 32; and Negro Society for Historical Research, 32; "Marcus Garvey Must Go," 34; in American Negro Academy, 34; among Ferris' "12 Greatest Negroes," 37; *Negro World* contrasts to Marcus Garvey, 38; accused of plagiarism, 38-39; complaints by Hubert H. Harrison, 39;

sculpted by Augusta Savage, 68; and Mary White Ovington, 94; attacks *Home to Harlem*, 137, 162; on Garvey's physical features, 161; on Liberty Hall, 161; satirizes Garvey in *Dark Princess*, 161-63; literary borrowings from J.A. Rogers, 163
Dumas, Alexandre, 128
Dunbar, Paul Laurence, 9, 15, 20, 47, 64, 88, 119, 128; works recited by Amy Ashwood Garvey, 3
Dunbar Players, 119, 121
Dunlap, Ethel Trew, 50-57, 58, 76, 87, 159

Eason, J. W. H., 29
Eclectic Club, 36, 74
Edelweis Park, 113
Egypt, 73, 110, 153, 155
Emperor Jones (O'Neill), 10, 93, 116, 117, 162, 164; reactions at Harlem premiere, 118; James Weldon Johnson compares Garvey to, 161
England, 3, 63-64, 79, 133, 136
Este, Charles H. D., 31, 44, 62
Ethiopia, 56, 57, 64, 72-73, 107, 108, 109, 135, 152; Garvey's poems on, 153-54. *See also* Abyssinia
Evening Transcript (Boston), 16, 18

Fauset, Jessie, 18, 91, 117; on propaganda, 16; *There is Confusion*, 20
Ferris, William H., 5, 14, 15, 20, 22, 26, 30, 34, 35, 37, 39, 4 2,

47, 64, 86, 91, 94, 103, 105, 112, 115, 116-17, 130, 134, 156, 163; on propaganda, 13; contributing editor, *Weekly Review*, 29; and Niagara Movement, 32; in American Negro Academy, 33; "Twelve Greatest Negroes," 37; accuses DuBois of plagiarism, 38; judge for literary contest, 40; eulogizes Lucian B. Watkins, 67-68; *The African Abroad*, 80; on *Batouala*, 95, 96-97; debate with T. Thomas Fortune, 121-22; photo, 85

Fire!!, 69

Flaming Sword, The (Dixon), 159-60

Ford, Arnold J., 106, 107, 108-09, 159; *Universal Ethiopian Hymnal*, 108

Ford, Henry, 128

Fortune, T. Thomas, 5, 28, 86, 156; editor, *Daily Negro Times*, 35; parody of Kipling, 81; debate with Ferris, 121-22; on Garvey's poetry, 140

Frazier, E. Franklin, 15

From Peasant to Crown Prince of Egypt, 113

From Superman to Man (Rogers), 30, 93, 99-101, 102, 163

Garnet, Henry Highland, 117

Garvey, Amy Ashwood (wife No. 1), 3; meets Marcus Garvey, 4; *Hey! Hey!, Brown Sugar, Black Magic*, 113

Garvey, Amy Jacques (wife No.

2), 15, 42, 105, 132; *Philosophy and Opinions of Marcus Garvey*, 14, 105; "Whither Goest Thou?", 14; praises Langston Hughes, 18-19; *The Tragedy of White Injustice, Selections from the Poetic Meditations of Marcus Garvey*, 144; Garvey's poem to, 147; photo 84

Garvey, Julius Winston, 147

Garvey, Marcus, 29, 80-81, 94, 115, 116, 117, 122, 133, 135, 156, 157, 159, 164; photo at Bruce funeral, vi; "rediscovered" by Black movement, 1; biographical sketch, 2-7; as journalist, 3; "The West Indies in the Mirror of Truth," 4; *A Talk With Afro-West Indians*, 4; as poet, 7; "African Fundamentalism," 9, 140; attacks *Home to Harlem*, 10, 15-16, 137; criticizes Paul Robeson, 10, 117-18; and propaganda in art, 14; as educator, 25; policy towards aspiring writers, 26; effect on Liberty Hall audience, 28; tries to launch *Blackman* (1922), 30; *Philosophy and Opinions of Marcus Garvey*, 31, 105; contrasted with DuBois, 38; subject of literary competition, 39; judge for literary competition, 40; his quotations as wall cards, 42; subject of *Negro World* poets, 45-46, 54, 62; sculpted by Augusta Savage, 68-69; attracts Poston brothers, 71; eulogizes R. L. Poston, 72; satirized by Zora Neale Hurston, 75-76; Carl Van Vechten on, 77; poem to, by J. E. Bruce, 86; arrest, conviction, deportation, 89-90; speaks at Liberty League meeting, 92; and beginnings of *Negro World*, 101-02; "God Bless our President," 107; song writer, 107-08; *UNIA Convention Hymns*, 108, 144, 149; poems set to music, 108; playright, 113; *The Coronation of the African King*, 113; as character in play, 114; *Grand Speech of Hon. Marcus Garvey ... Denouncing the Moving Picture Propaganda to Discredit the Negro*, 118; projected satire, *Jeremiah the Magnificent*, 118; collects African artwork, 120; and elocution, 120; debates communist, 123; attacked by Walrond, 129-31; and Walrond, in England, 132; exchanges with McKay, 136; as poet, 139-55; writes poetry in Atlanta, 139; his library, 140; "If I Die in Atlanta," 140-44; on Black nationalism, 143; *Selections from the Poetic Meditations of Marcus Garvey*, 144; *The Tragedy, of White Injustice*, 78, 144, 145-46, 148, 150, 151, 152, 154; poem to Amy Jacques Garvey, 147; religion in his poems,

149-50; on United States of Africa, 152; poems on Black history, 153-54; as literary and artistic symbol, 159-63; as "religious" figure, 159; national hero of Jamaica, 160; compared to Emperor Jones by J. W. Johnson, 161; DuBois on his physical features, 161; satirized in DuBois' *Dark Princess*, 161-63; interest in literature and the arts, 163

Garvey aesthetic, 8-24, 109, 111, 122, 157, 160, 163, 164. *See also* Black aesthetic

Ghana, 44, 65. *See also* Gold Coast

Gilpin, Charles, 10, 11, 12, 117

Gold, Michael, 136

Gold Coast, 44. *See also* Ghana

Gold Coast Leader, 65, 89

Goncourt prize, 95

Grand Speech of Hon. Marcus Garvey ... (Garvey), 118

Gray, Arthur S., 12

Grenada, 44, 77, 124

Grimké, Archibald H., 37

Grimké, Francis L., 37

Guardian (Boston), 39

Guatemala, 44

Haiti, 152

Hamitic League of the World, 80

Hammon, Jupiter, 57

Harlem, 5, 32, 34, 35, 37, 69, 74, 92, 98, 113, 116, 118, 161, 164; sketches of life in, by Zora Neale Hurston, 73

Harlem Renaissance, inadequate precedent for

Black Arts Movement , 1;
white mentors of, 18; former
Negro World writers in, 27;
influenced by Maran, 99

Harlem Shadows (McKay), 36,
93, 134

Harper, N. R., *Tallaboo*, 115

Harris, A. Lincoln, 114, 116

Harris, Frank, 46, 133

Harris, George W., 35

Harrison, Hubert H., 5, 26, 34,
39, 67, 86, 92-93, 94, 95, 98,
100, 102 , 105, 115, 117, 156,
157, 164; criticized by *Negro
World* reader, 11-12; book
review pioneer, 91; as
discoverer and nurturer of
Black talent, 132-33.

Harvard University, 5, 102, 115

Hayford, J. E. Casely, 65

Haynes, S. A., 103

Haywood, Harry, 80

Henry, Thomas Millard, 66

Hey! Hey!, 113

History of the Negro Church
(Woodson), 103

Ho Chi Minh, 45

Hollywood, 119

Holstein, Casper, 41

Home to Harlem (McKay), 16;
attacked by Garvey, 10, 137;
attacked by DuBois, 137

Houston, Mme M. B., 108

Howard University, 70, 73

Howells, William Dean, 9

Huggins, Willis N., 37

Hughes, Langston, 24, 35, 69,
106, 129; praised by Amy
Jacques Garvey, 18-19

Hugo, Victor, 93

Hurston, Zora Neale, x, 18, 26,
27, 36, 41, 66, 69, 73-77, 125,
131, 156, 158, 160, 164;
satirizes Garvey, 75-76

Independent, The, 130

India, 110

International Conventions of the
Negro Peoples of the World,
30; 1921, 71; Woman's Day,
1921, 31; proposal to commission a history of Black
literature, 1924, 30; 1929, 123;
1934, 108

Isles, William, 106, 108, 109-12

Jackson School of Music, 36

Jacques, Amy. *See* Amy
Jacques Garvey

Jamaica, 2, 3, 44, 63, 89, 99,
106, 120, 123, 149, 160

Jamaica Times, 136

Jefferson, Thomas, 50

Jeremiah the Magnificent
(Thurman and Rapp), 118, 160

Jews, 103. *See also* Black Jews

Johnson, Charles S., 6

Johnson, Fenton, 4, 37, 58

Johnson, James Weldon, 29, 32,
39, 106, 131, 161; criticized by
Negro World, 22; *The Book of
American Negro Poetry*, 30,
68; and American Negro
Academy, 34

Jones, Madame Maud, 121

Journal of Negro History, 102

Jubilee music, 110-11, 112

Julius Caesar (Shakespeare), 28

Kerlin, Robert., 67

King, Martin Luther, 142-44

Kipling, Rudyard, 17, 81

Kirnon, Hodge, 101
Ku Klux Klan, 45, 73
Krigwa Players Little Negro Theatre, 156

Lafayette Theatre, 116
Lakey, Marion S., 8, 57
Leonard, William Ellery, 94
Lewis, Robert Benjamin, 31
Liberator, 23, 132, 134, 135, 136; *Liberator* Costume Ball, 135
Liberia, 44, 72, 152
Liberty Hall, 72, 106, 109, 113, 115, 121, 122, 134; negative description by DuBois, 161
Liberty Hall Choir, 106
Liberty League, 92
Light and Truth (Lewis), 31
Lincoln, Abraham, 93, 142
Lindsay, Rev. C. Anthony, 40
Literary clubs, 31
Literary contests, x; 1921, *Negro World*, 39-41, 44, 156; *Crisis* and *Opportunity*, 39
Locke, Alain, 4, 26, 95, 96, 158-59; *The New Negro*, 6, 68; former *Negro World* authors in *The New Negro*, 156
L'Ouverture, Toussaint, 46, 117
Lowell, James Russell, 93
Lynching Bee and Other Poems, The (Leonard), 94

Mair, Ernest E., 62-64, 69, 86-87
Maloney, Arnold Hamilton, 25, 26, 156; in American Negro Academy, 33; *Some Essentials of Race Leadership*, 105
Maran, René, 94-99; *Batouala*, 27, 30, 95-99, 127

March on Washington, 142
"Marcus Garvey Must Go," 6, 35
Marryshow, T. Albert, 77
Matthews, Estella, 87
McKay, Claude, 9, 36, 46, 63, 74, 120, 131, 132-38, 156, 159, 164; on Marcus Garvey, 6-7; *Home to Harlem*, 10, 16, 137; and white mentors, 18; *The Negroes in America*, 22; on propaganda, 22-23; "If We Must Die," 24; *Harlem Shadows*, 36, 93, 134; *A Long Way From Home*, 101; *Spring in New Hampshire*, 133; satirized in *Negro World*, 135-36; exchange with Garvey in media, 136; defends Garvey in *New York Times*, 138; attacked by DuBois, 162
McLean, McDonald, 29
Mesopotamia, 110
Messenger, x, 6, 156
Mexico, 44
Miller, Kelly, 38, 100
Minor and Patterson, 98
Mis-Education of the Negro, The (Woodson), 105
Moton, Robert Russa, 129
Mudgal, H. G., 12, 81, 86, 122-123; on Rudyard Kipling, 17
Murray, Daniel, 31; in Negro Library Association of New York City, 32
Murray's Historical and Biographical Encyclopaedia of the Colored Race Throughout the World (Murray), 31
Music Trade News, 108
Mussolini, Benito, 153

Mystery of Space (Browne), 38

National Association for the Advancement of Colored People (NAACP), 10, 32, 33, 34, 39, 94, 100, 126, 161
Native Life in South Africa (Plaatje), 30, 39
National Equal Rights League, 39
"Nefertari," 136
Negritude, 80
Negro History Week, 102
Negro In Art and Literature, The (Brawley), 30
Negro In Our History, The (Woodson), 103
Negro Library Association of New York City, 32, 33
Negro Society for Historical Research, 5, 32, 33, 104
Negro World, ix, x, 8, 9, 10, 11, 12, 16, 187; early history, 4-5; editors, 5, 32, 156; against *Emperor Jones*, 10-12; criticizes DuBois and J. W. Johnson, 21-22; and literature, 25, 27; its writers in wider Harlem scene, 32; editorial against Ernestine Rose, 35; visitors to office of, 37; favorable to *Opportunity*, 38; contrasts Garvey and DuBois, 38; bumper 1921 Christmas number, 39-42; and propaganda in art, 41; poetry, 43-90; considers anthology of its verse, 89; book reviews, 91-105; banned in West Indies, Africa and Latin America, 65, 146; its writers

in Locke's *New Negro*, 156; as infrastructure for Harlem Renaissance, 156; circulation, 156; literary contest, 1921, x, 39-41, 44, 156
Negroes in America, The (McKay), 22
New Negro, The (Harris), 114, 116
New Negro, The (Locke), 6, 7, 68; *Negro World* writers in, 156
New Republic, 39, 129, 131
New York News, 35
New York Public Library (135th St.), 34, 68, 93, 129. *See also* Schomburg Center for Research in Black Culture
New York Times, 92, 137, 138
New York University, 92
Niagara Movement, 32, 38
Nigeria, 44, 89, 115
Nigger Heaven (Van Vechten), 19-20, 76-77, 160
Nkrumah, Kwame, 78
Nubia, 153
Nurse, H. A., 56

Odds and Ends Tea Room, 37
Olivier, Sir Sidney, 135
O'Meally, James, 136
O'Neill, Eugene, 11, 93, 161
Opportunity, x, 6, 25, 38, 39, 41, 130, 131, 156
Ovington, Mary White, 91, 93-94, 95, 96, 127; *The Shadow*, 94
Owen, Chandler, 6

Palmer, A. Mitchell, 90
Pan-African Congress, 126

Pan-Africanism, 152

Panama, 3, 29, 40, 44, 124

Parker, George Wells, 80-81;
Children of the Sun, 80

Pearson's Magazine, 10, 46, 133

Perigua, Mr., 161-62

Perry, Rev. Rufus L., 31

Peterson, Sadie, 35, 36, 68, 129

Philosophy and Opinions of Marcus Garvey (Garvey), 14, 31, 165

Phyllis Wheatley, S. S. (ship), 47

Phyllis Wheatley Hotel, 36, 48

Pickens, William, 29, 34;
Vengeance of the Gods, 93

Pittsburgh Courier, 12

Plaatje, Solomon, *Native Life in South Africa*, 30, 39, 133

Plantation Revue, The, 116

Plummer, E. V., 34

Poe, Edgar Allan, 93

Poston, Robert Lincoln, 70-73, 86, 91, 102-03, 112, 115, 156;
on McKay, 23; funeral of, 72-73

Poston, Roberta L., 73

Poston, Ulysses S., 34, 71-72, 115-16, 156

Preaching vs. Practice (Bruce), 114

Propaganda, 12-18, 41, 113

Pushkin, Alexander, 128, 132

Randolph, A. Philip, 6

Rapp, Willard Jourdan, 118, 160

Rastafarians, 149

Reeves, Sir William Conrad, 117

Reid, B. de C., 108

Republican Party, 5

Rising Tide of Color Against White Supremacy, The (Stoddard), 62

Robeson, Paul, 10, 117-18, 164

Rockefeller foundation, 102

Rogers, J. A., x, 26, 36, 37, 80, 91, 94, 95, 96, 99-102, 133, 156, 158, 164; *From Superman to Man*, 30, 93, 99-101, 102, 163; *As Nature Leads*, 93, 102; on *Batouala*, 97-98; DuBois "borrows" from, 163

Rose, Ernestine, 35-36, 129

Sanborn, Gertrude, 37

Sanders of the River, 117

Savage, Augusta, 35, 66, 68-70, 73, 106, 120, 129, 159; busts of Garvey and DuBois, 68-69

Scarborough, William S., 37, 100

Schomburg, Arthur A., x, 26, 35, 36, 91, 100, 102, 103-104, 129, 156; photo at Bruce funeral, vi; in American Negro Academy, 33; supporter of Garvey, 33; in Negro Library Association of New York City, 32; accuses DuBois of plagiarism, 39; library in Brooklyn, 73-74

Schomburg Center for Research in Black Culture, 34. *See also* New York Public Library (135th St.)

Schomburg Center for Research in Black Culture, 34. *See also* New York Public Library (135th St.)

Schuyler, George S., 123, 146

Sekyi, Kobina, 77-80

Selections from the Poetic Meditations of Marcus Garvey (Garvey), 144
Semper, Mrs. Maud, 107
Seven Arts, 10
Seymour, Alexander, 108
Shadow, The (Ovington), 94
Shakespeare, William, 15, 20, 47, 119, 121; *Julius Caesar, 28*
Shuffle Along, 116, 117
Sidney, Sir Philip, 140
Sierra Leone, 124
Siki, Battling, 64
Simon the Cyrenian, 149
Slave songs, 110-11, 112
Socialist Party, 92
Some Essentials of Race Leadership (Maloney), 105
South Africa, 159
South African Native National Congress, 39
Soviet Union, 22
Spring in New Hampshire (McKay), 133
Stevedore, 117
Star and Herald, 29
St. Croix, 92
Stoddard, Lothrop, 62
Stowe, Harriet Beecher, 13
Stribling, T. S., 27, 127
Strut Miss Lizzie, 116
St. Thomas, 104
Stuart-Young, J.M., 88-89, 93; *What Does It Matter?*, 89
Sudan, 44
Survey, 35

Tallaboo (Harper), 115-16, 119

Tanner, Henry O., 38
Taylor, Lester, 36, 115
There is Confusion (Fauset), 20
Third World Press, 1
Thomas, Norton G., 28
Thurman, Wallace, 69, 118, 160
Toomer, Jean, 20, 21, 131
Tragedy of White Injustice, The (Garvey), 144, 145-46, 148, 150, 151, 152, 154
Trench and Camp Magazine, 73
Trinidad, 160
Tropic Death (Walrond), 131, 132
Trotter, William Monroe, 38-39, 100, 117
Turner, Bishop Henry McNeal, 50
Tuskegee Institute, 126, 129
Tut-Ankh-Amen, Pharoah, 113
Twenty-Four Negro Melodies (Coleridge-Taylor), 111

Ubangui-Shari, 95
Uncle Tom's Cabin (Stowe), 13
UNIA. See Universal Negro Improvement Association
United States Canal Zone, 44
United States of Africa, 152
Universal African Legions, 72, 107
Universal Choir, 106
Universal Ethiopian Anthem, 107, 108, 109
Universal Follies, 106
Universal Jazz Hounds, 106, 109
Universal Negro Improvement Association, 19, 40, 124; as precursor to 1960s generation, 2; membership, 2,

21; Jamaican beginnings, 3; literary censor suggested at 1924 and 1934 conventions, 17; contributions to literature, 25ff. and passim; and *Weekly Review*, 29; literary clubs in, 31, 44; in Dominica, 31; in Montreal, 31, 44; in Jamaica, 31; in Boston, 31; in Portland, Oregon, 31; in Santiago, Cuba, 32; in Norfolk and Newport News, Va., 32; intellectual substance of, 33; Montreal literary club, 44; poems to, 45; in Detroit, 77; in Indianapolis, 106; in Harlem, 106, 113; in Philadelphia, 114; women, 84

Universal Negro Improvement Association Convention Hymns (Garvey), 144, 149
Universal Negro Improvement Association Convention Hymns (Garvey), 144, 149
Universal Negro Improvement Association Dramatic Club, 83, 115, 119, 156
Universal Negro Improvement Association Publishing House, 31
Upreach Magazine, 37

Van Der Zee, James, 120, 159
Van Doren, Carl, 35
Van Vechten, Carl, 75, 77; *Nigger Heaven*, 19-20, 76-77, 160
Veiled Aristocrats (Sanborn), 37
Vengeance of the Gods (Pickens), 93
Venezuela, 44, 47

Vesey, Denmark, 104
Virgin Islands, 41
Voice, The, 92

Walden University, 70
Walrond, Eric D., x, 5, 27, 35, 36, 37, 39, 68, 74, 76, 91, 92, 93, 95, 98, 125-32, 156, 158, 161; on propaganda, 16-17; associate editor of *Weekly Review*, 29; prizewinner, *Negro World* literary contest, 40-41; attacks Garvey, 129-31; *Tropic Death*, 131; and Garvey, in England, 132
Ward, Theodore, 161
Washington, Booker T., 4, 5, 47
Watkins, Lucian B., 66-68, 156
Weekly Review, 29
West Africa, 89
West Indians, 35, 39, 47, 63, 131, 162
What Does It Matter? (Stuart-Young), 89
Wheatley, Phillis, 46, 47, 48-50, 139
White, Walter, 131
White Peacock, The, 37
Whittier, John Greenleaf, 23, 46
Wilberforce University, 25
Williams, Geneva, 56
Williams, John S., 53
Woman question, in poetry, 86-88; Garvey's poems on, 150; UNIA women, 84
Women's Day, 31
Woodson, Carter G., 102-04, 156, 158; accuses DuBois of plagiarism, 39; *The Negro In Our History*, 103-04; *History of the Negro Church*, 103;

publishes in *Negro World*,
104-05; *The Mis-Education of
the Negro*, 105
Wordsworth, William, 46
Workers (Communist) Party of
the U.S.A., 134-35
Wright, Richard, 77

Yale University, 5, 99, 115